ABOUT *The Bayberry Bush*

INGRID SCHAFFNER
WITH MELISSA FELDMAN

THE PARRISH ART MUSEUM
SOUTHAMPTON, NEW YORK

DONORS

This project has been made possible with generous support from:

THE WILLIAM ROSENWALD FAMILY FUND, INC.

ROBERT M. RUBIN AND STEPHANE B. SAMUEL

ARTHUR LOEB FOUNDATION

DR. AND MRS. WERNER OTTO

THE TIGHE HIDALGO FAMILY

HERMAN GOLDMAN FOUNDATION

LINDA AND GREGORY FISCHBACH

DEL LABORATORIES

CHRISTIE'S

ROBERT LEHMAN FOUNDATION, INC.

HELENE STEVENS

HUGH J. FREUND

ELLEN AND JEROME STERN

Published in conjunction with the exhibition
About the Bayberry Bush
The Parrish Art Museum
July 29 – October 14, 2001

CONTENTS

FOREWORD AND ACKNOWLEDGMENTS

I AM ALWAYS ASTONISHED at how exhibition ideas materialize. For many years now, curators and artists have been looking at the past through museum collections and works of art, and organizing presentations that have established unforgettable connections between past and present. Memorable examples include Fred Wilson's *Mining the Museum,* at The Contemporary and Maryland Historical Society, Baltimore (1992); Chuck Close's *Artist's Choice: Head-on/The Modern Portrait,* at the Museum of Modern Art (1991); and the Parrish's own *A Museum Looks at Itself: Mapping Past and Present at The Parrish Art Museum, 1897–1992* (1992).

A museum like the Parrish, whose collection is grounded in a sense of place, has an enduring commitment to those artists whose perceptions capture the defining qualities of the light and landscape of the eastern end of Long Island. Our holdings of William Merritt Chase and Fairfield Porter are substantial and legendary: two artists whose visions of place span almost a century and are cherished by visitors and residents alike. As we contemplated how the museum might celebrate its collection, in anticipation of its installation in a new building, a young and talented curator, Ingrid Schaffner, came to mind as the person to take on the challenge.

My talks with Ingrid, together with Alicia Longwell, curator at the Parrish, were lively, even funny. Ingrid acknowledges in her introduction that she noticed a reproduction of a Chase painting in my office during our discussions, but it was not until she viewed the museum's collection that this seminal work, *The Bayberry Bush,* struck her as inspiration for an exhibition.

Many distinguished scholars have explored Chase, among them the Parrish's former director and curator Ronald G. Pisano, whose pioneering efforts led the way for others. Ingrid's notion of inviting contemporary artists to interpret Chase was refreshing and thoughtful, even though we recognized there might be risks. Collaborating with Ingrid was Melissa Feldman, and we are extremely grateful to have had the breadth of her knowledge too in selecting artists and organizing the exhibition.

We are fortunate that the artists from around the world who agreed to respond to a nineteenth-century American Impressionist painting surpassed all our expectations for bringing different perspectives and media to bear on this treasured work. It has been an honor to unite this distinguished group: Richard Artschwager, Knut Åsdam, Bonnie Collura, Peter Doig, Joseph Grigely, Jitka Hanzlová, Joan Jonas, Lee Mingwei, José Alejandro Restrepo, Beverly Semmes, and Yutaka Sone. An artist's interpretation of historical material, or in fact any material, should evolve without restraint, and thus we regret being unable to present Cai Guo-Qiang's project, because of concerns over the safety and well-being of live animals and the public in the museum setting.

Our curators ranged far and wide to locate the diversity and richness of imagination that can be employed in considering a work of art. We are especially privileged to read the haunting verses conjured by the poet Linda Bierds after Chase's painting; a thoroughgoing analysis of the work by the art historian Sarah Burns, Ruth N. Halls Professor at Indiana University, Bloomington; and the specific observations of a number of individuals that enhance our view of *The Bayberry Bush:* Elizabeth Haile, Richard Hendrickson, Dr. Stephen Leatherman, Dr. Stuart Lowrie, David Bunn Martine, Dr. Gaynell Stone, Dr. John Strong, and Dr. Robert Turner.

An exhibition of this magnitude depends on the generosity of parties who share with us the adventure of exploring a new concept. We have enjoyed the kind support of The William Rosenwald Family Fund, Inc., Robert M. Rubin and Stephane B. Samuel, Dr. and Mrs. Werner Otto, The Tighe Hidalgo Family, Herman Goldman Foundation, Linda and Gregory Fischbach,

Del Laboratories, Inc., Christie's, the Robert Lehman Foundation, Inc., Helene Stevens, Hugh J. Freund, and Ellen and Jerome Stern. We are especially grateful to Arthur Loeb for underwriting the publication of the catalogue.

We are grateful likewise to the galleries and artists' assistants who unfailingly facilitated our curators' needs and desires: Ann Artschwager; Sekeena Gavagan; Jennifer Ma and Hong Hong Wu; and in New York City: Lehmann Maupin Gallery; Kirsty Bell and Gavin Brown at Gavin Brown's enterprise; Cohan Leslie and Browne; Klemens Gasser and Tanja Grunert at Klemens Gasser & Tanja Grunert; Pat Hearn Gallery; Lea Freid at Lombard-Freid Fine Arts; and Hanna Schouwink at David Zwirner Gallery.

Central to this enterprise has been the skilled team that helped shape the catalogue, presentation, education offerings, underwriting, and public relations. Many thanks to Anna Jardine for her editorial intelligence; to Bethany Johns for the beauty of the book's design; to Barbara Suhr for her expert command of the exhibition material; to Cathy Carver for photography; to Ruder Finn, Arts and Communication Counselors, for promoting this endeavor; and to Leah Buechley for her ongoing diligence and assistance. Among the Parrish staff, we owe a special debt of gratitude to Alicia Longwell, Curator of Art; Christine McNamara, Registrar; Novella Laspia, Curatorial Assistant; Cara Conklin-Wingfield, Educator for School Programs; Susan Jordan, Educator for Public Programs; Sally Briggs, Director of Development; Anke Jackson, Deputy Director; and Erin Ferguson, Director of Public Relations.

Equally vital have been our Trustees. Guided by the steady hand of Chairman Mildred Brinn, they encourage and support our meanderings, yet remain mindful of the importance of an artistic legacy rich in meaning and treasured by many here and beyond.

TRUDY C. KRAMER
Director, The Parrish Art Museum

ABOUT *The Bayberry Bush*

THE STORY OF THIS EXHIBITION begins in March 1999, with what seemed to be an American Impressionist landscape I saw leaning near the radiator in the office of Trudy Kramer, the director of the Parrish Art Museum. Located in the historic resort town of Southampton, on Long Island, the Parrish serves a region famous for attracting artists—Jackson Pollock, Andy Warhol, Chuck Close, Julian Schnabel, and Cindy Sherman notable among them—as summer, or even year-round, residents. But this was winter, and the radiator was hissing away at the painting. How to be tactful? "Tell me about *that*," I asked Kramer, pointing to the nineteenth-century canvas baking in its gold frame. "Oh, that's the museum's most important picture—*The Bayberry Bush*, by William Merritt Chase. It was done around 1895, just a few miles from here, in the Shinnecock Hills, where Chase ran one of the first schools of outdoor painting in the country. Our visitors are constantly asking to see it. But we don't have the gallery space. That's one of the reasons for the museum's upcoming expansion: to keep the permanent collection on view." My expression of puzzled horror prompted Kramer to add, "This isn't the real painting, of course. It's only a reproduction on canvas—something to consider for gift-shop sales."

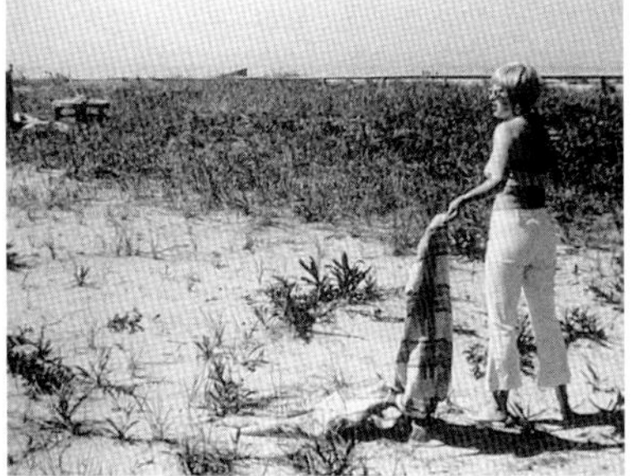

Cindy Sherman, *Untitled Film Still #8*, 1978. Gelatin silver print, 8 x 10 inches.

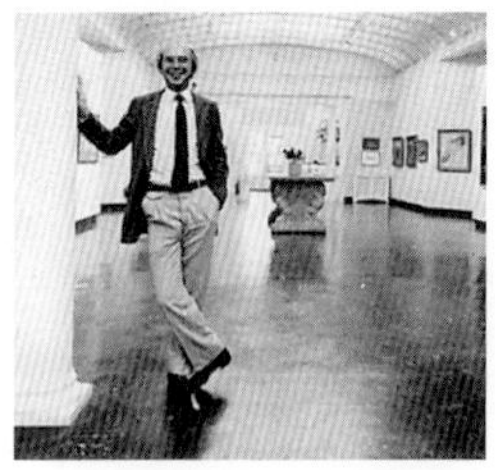

Ronald G. Pisano, Chase scholar and former director of The Parrish Art Museum, 1980.

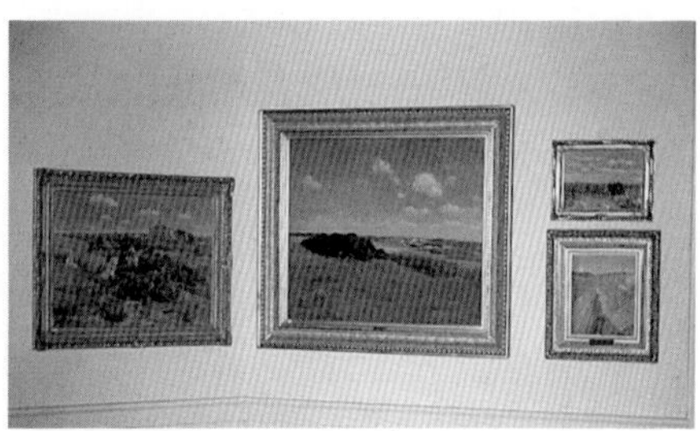

The Parrish Art Museum galleries, c. 1965. Installation of works by Chase in the collection.

Later that afternoon, while touring the Parrish with curator Alicia Longwell, I encountered the real *Bayberry Bush,* secured on a rack in a climate-controlled storage area. It was surrounded by other works of Chase's, as well as those of artists who had lived or summered on the eastern end of Long Island after him. Upstairs, in a storeroom for prints and drawings, we looked at photographs from the Chase Archives, initiated in the 1970s by the Chase scholar and former Parrish director Ronald Pisano as a resource for historians and others. There were pictures of the artist and his children taken in the area, Victorian summer-holiday snapshots. "Chase's wife, Alice Gerson, was an amateur photographer. We have postcards of hers ordering chemicals for her home darkroom," Longwell told me. The family evidently enjoyed dressing up in costumes and staging *tableaux vivants,* or living pictures, after historic works of art. In a nod to one of his heroes in art, Chase appears all duded up in pseudo-seventeenth-century Dutch attire, complete with ruff collar, and featuring a clay pipe and other props, fit to be painted by Frans Hals.

But back to the radiator. The purpose of my visit and meeting with Kramer and Longwell that winter day in 1999 was to discuss a project for summer 2001. They wanted a show about landscape (to

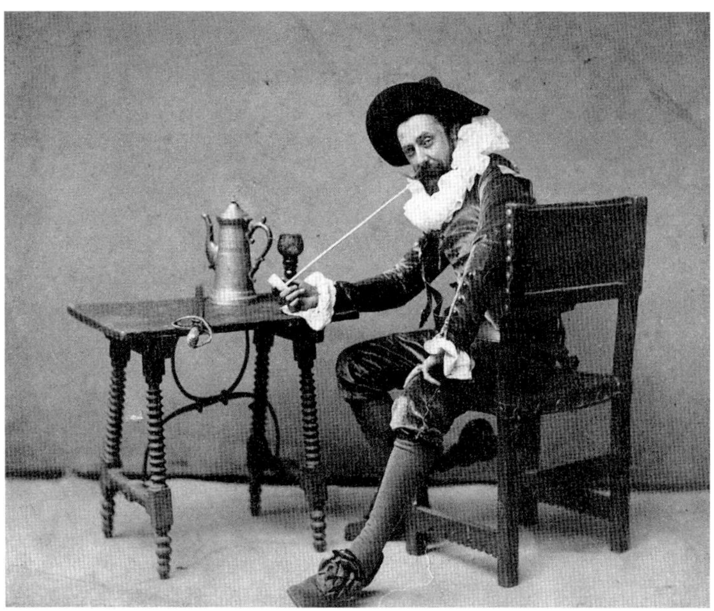

Chase dressed for a costume ball, posed after *The Smoker* by Frank Duveneck, c. 1886. Gelatin printing-out paper, 7 x 9 inches, mounted on cardboard. The William Merritt Chase Archives, The Parrish Art Museum, Gift of Jackson Chase Storm.

reinforce the museum's association with that tradition) that might have a more global impact (to reflect the interests of the contemporary art world). With these considerations, I was asked to propose a theme for an exhibition, and as I contemplated the possibilities, one picture, emblematic of the local landscape and history, and beloved of the collection, asserted itself: William Merritt Chase's *The Bayberry Bush*.

Whatever one's personal tastes, it would be difficult not to respond to this painting. Set (and made) in the Gilded Age, it evokes a distant but tangible period of prosperity and transition from Victorian to modern times. The painter's loose, open brushwork conveys the immediacy of working outdoors and being in the landscape, where three little girls in white frocks play around the eponymous bush. Ribbons in their bonnets sing out the primary colors: red, yellow, and blue. Scrubby dunes radiate warmth beneath a sparkling blue sky, filled with sun and dotted with puffy white clouds. In the distance stands a grand summer house, under a large gambrel roof, an example of the Shingle Style that is a standard in coastal real estate even today. The scene is an American vacation idyll, but the picture transmits more widely by way of its Impressionism. What originated in France during the later nineteenth century has spawned historic schools and a style of painting from the Americas to Australia, from China to Mexico. Wherever aspirations for Western culture exist, Impressionism is to be found. It reinforces the meaning of the image, down to the pigment and canvas—never mind the gold frame! *The Bayberry Bush,* like many another Impressionist work, speaks loudly and prettily of leisure, refinement, affluence, and family values in bourgeois society.

At least, that's essentially what I conceived it would do in the context of this project: that, and trigger responses from contemporary artists who would be commissioned by the Parrish to create new work for an exhibition about *The Bayberry Bush*. To help select and organize the commissions, I called on my colleague Melissa Feldman, with whom I had collaborated on *Secret Victorians: Contemporary Art and a Nineteenth-Century Vision*. This project, like that one, would operate in dual drive, shifting between a previous turn of the century and now. Together we set out to select twelve artists, who would offer the museum installation-scale works. We wanted a group that would represent a range of experiences and practices. This meant artists not only with different national perspectives, but also of different ages, at various points in their careers, and working in a variety of media. We considered their individual approaches as critical to creating a good mix. Some were invited because their work shared imagery or themes with Chase's painting, while others were asked because their work spectacularly opposed it. The catalogue entries that follow discuss the curatorial process as it relates to each of the artists: Richard Artschwager, Knut Åsdam, Cai Guo-Qiang, Bonnie Collura, Peter Doig, Joseph Grigely, Jitka Hanzlová, Joan Jonas, Lee Mingwei, José Alejandro Restrepo, Beverly Semmes, and Yutaka Sone.

As simple as it may sound, arriving at our selection was no straightforward matter. I am based in New York, and Melissa is now in Washington, D.C., after five years in London; between us, we share access to an international scene. But in recent years the art world has greatly expanded. To represent global perspectives, as this exhibition seeks to do, is more and more a challenge when artists are surfacing everywhere and art fairs are opening in Havana, Taipei, and points between. Covering this world is a new breed of nomadic colleagues, for whom a commute from Johannesburg to Istanbul, Kassel to Seoul, Venice to Pittsburgh, is all in a day's work. Fortunately, the exhibitions being organized in far-flung places produce catalogues, which can in fact be used as such. As we paged through these publications, we were introduced to many potential candidates, and to the armchair method of international curating, which involves the works of well-documented (and well-traveled) artists. At the same time, we tried to be aware of, and avoid, inducing the state of creative jet-lag to which people who are invited to be in too many places at once are susceptible. In tracking down our catalogue discoveries, we were amused to learn that most had New York addresses or affiliations. This isn't so surprising, with the art market flourishing here; but it is paradoxical that the wider the (Western) world casts its net, the more centralized culture seems to become. And yet finding Manhattan to be the center of the art world somewhat lessened our anxieties about not having seen the most recent show held in, say, Ljubljana.

This is not to imply that the world was our oyster. To put it plainly, as pretty, academic, and safe as *The Bayberry Bush* is, it is the antithesis of contemporary art, which often aims to critique, tweak, or undermine those very qualities. And there is that aspect of the project which sounds like an assignment, imposing too particular a goal on studio time, which is intrinsically about having the freedom to do whatever you want. One artist, when invited, simply informed us no, thank you, he didn't think about other art when he made his work. Fair enough. Some artists immediately took to the idea; others had the inclination, but not the time; some rejected the project outright; others eventually came around. In the end, the selection was very much an organic process, shaped as much by our own efforts as by those of curatorial colleagues, writers, artists, and dealers, among whom we especially thank Stefano Basilico, Carlos Basualdo, Geoffrey Batchen, Thom Collins, Anne Doran, Elizabeth Finch, Lea Freid, Dana Friis-Hansen, Robert Gober, Laura Hoptman, Carin Kuoni, Barry Schwabsky, Lori Toppel, and Jolie van Leeuwen. Their support and advice were invaluable.

No matter how (or why) they were selected, artists were invited to respond without any expectation from us about what they would produce. They could work as usual, or take a holiday, a summer holiday, from their normal practice and try something new. Each was equipped with photographic images of Chase's painting. And although they were encouraged to visit the Parrish to see the original, this wasn't deemed essential. (We live in an age of mechanical reproduction, after all.) Projects were supported by honoraria and a fixed sum toward fabrication, and all works are to remain the property of the artists. Each artist received a copy of the file, or dossier, that I compiled about elements in the Chase painting. Treating topics from archaeology to whaling, the dossier included research, copies of documents (such as the prospectus from the Shinnecock Summer School of Art, which Chase directed from 1891 to 1902), and material collected in interviews with local experts, including a botanist, a geologist, and a weatherman. (An edited version of the dossier appears as an appendix here.) The intent was to suggest ways of reading *The Bayberry Bush* that might offer conceptual points of engagement, or at least show that there is more to this

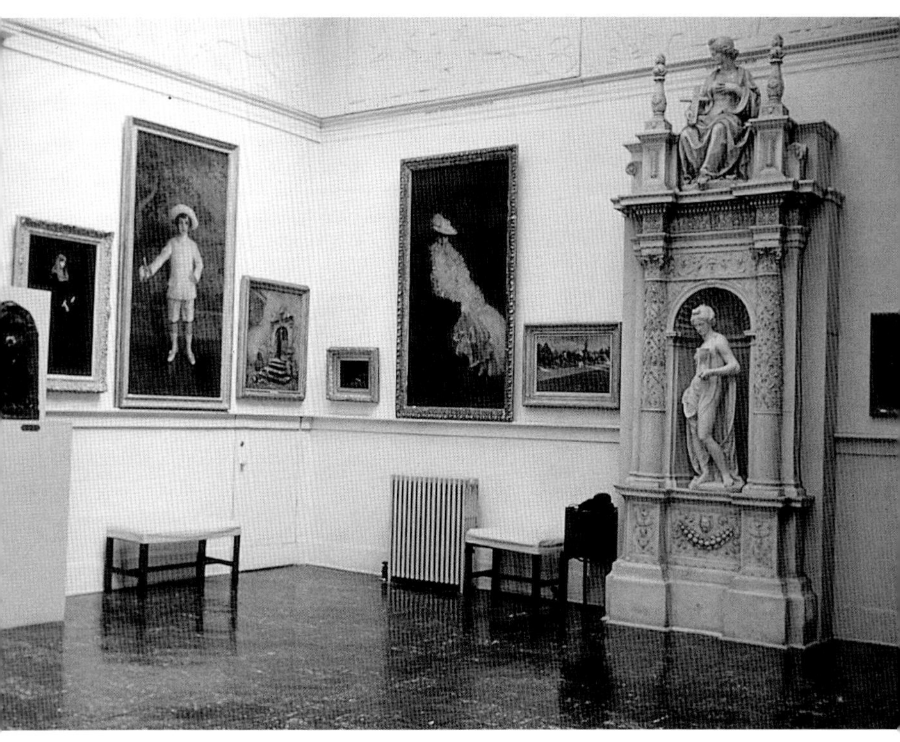

The Parrish Art Museum galleries, c. 1965. Installation of works by Chase in the collection.

picture than meets the eye. The Shinnecock Hills where the picture was painted, for example, are named for the indigenous people who were displaced to a nearby reservation in order to make way for the railroad and resorts, first built around the time of Chase's painting.

In addition to the dossier, artists received copies of catalogues of two past museum exhibitions: *Photographs from the William Merritt Chase Archives at The Parrish Art Museum* (1992) and *Past Imperfect: A Museum Looks at Itself* (1993). The former volume, compiled by Pisano and Longwell, is a marvel of the kind of close looking and deductive reasoning (which child? whose handwriting? what year?) it takes to transform piles of papers and pictures into working documents; indeed, it was the photographs in the Archives, more than Chase's painting, that inspired several of the artists. The latter, organized by Donna De Salvo, was a model of cultural criticism, art history, and innovative curatorial practice that set a high precedent for this book. In its examination of the institution at large, it also provided a foundation for our look at one picture in the museum's collection.

Granted, artists don't necessarily obtain their information from books and binders, which in this case they received with a caveat from the curators: "Take it or leave it." All were more or less interested, but as far as their process, many "left it"; one artist was hindered, another annoyed; a few were inspired and informed. The dossier may have been most useful to Linda Bierds, one of two writers commissioned to respond to *The Bayberry Bush* with a text. Bierds is a poet who frequently muses on works of art, and her writing process may involve extensive research about her subjects. In this instance, she clearly looked at, and then beyond, the information provided. Her lines touch on little-known facts about Chase's family around the time of the painting. The other writer is the art historian Sarah Burns, whose 1996 book *Inventing the Modern Artist: Art & Culture in Gilded Age America* put a new shine on Chase and the artists of his generation (Thomas Eakins, Cecilia Beaux, Winslow Homer, James Whistler, and others) in its discussion of such themes as healthy practice, strategic display, big business, and the hazards of femininity. Her essay here analyzes Chase the "human camera"—as he was hailed in his day—at work in the Shinnecock Hills. A third text, by curator Longwell, shows how the *tableau vivant,* that favorite pastime of the Chase family, is a perfect metaphor for the project of reanimating *The Bayberry Bush* through the perspectives of living artists.

At the time of this writing, with the exhibition several months away, the artists' installations are still very much works in progress. (A collection of postcard images documenting the completed installations is planned.) Herein lies this project's great risk, and its excitement: until the works actually arrive at the Parrish, there is no way of telling what the show will look like, what it will be. The project required preliminary proposals from all of the participants, which Melissa and I have reviewed, and on which we have based our entries; even as we write, some artists are revising their ideas. In any event, the forecast looks excellent, and comprises sculpture, painting, prints, sound, writing, ceramics, and, as might be expected a century and more from the summer day of Chase's painting, photography and video. What this promises—and what the catalogue texts and images that follow demonstrate—is that there is much to see, and say, about *The Bayberry Bush*.

INGRID SCHAFFNER
Guest Curator

FROM THE BAYBERRY BUSH

—after the painting by William Merritt Chase

LINDA BIERDS

Just before sunset, he will give to his young daughters
three dollops of oiled white—three brush flicks
straight from his palette to the melted wax

their bayberry berries have rendered. White candles, then,
begin with a wrist flick, one daughter will think,
though the pigment will float on the hot wax, stunned

for a moment, its cumulous shapes sweeping the surface
as the clouds do now, just over her bonneted head.
She is Alice, the eldest, facing her father

in the noon sun, facing his easel and peppered beard,
white pigment still on his brush tip, white berries
still on the bush. Hold, he tells her. And something

quickens within her. For an instant, her brother's face
in his infant's coffin. And the lost twins. Perhaps
they are sun spots, or berries white in the scrub,

those waxed faces flaring a moment, peripherally.
And then they are gone. Her father is laughing, afloat
in his own correspondences—how the house's gambreled

roof line, high on the painting's horizon, mimics
her bonnet's droop. And the windows
her steady gaze. How the static stirs, he thinks,

and the animate seeps to inanimacy. She is Alice,
his daughter, in a thicket of switchgrass and scruff,
linseed and tint. And now she is crossing

the kitchen floor, while the bayberry candles harden.
How clever, she tells him, that *bay* can be water or leaf.
And a bay's berries . . . like seeds from the sea!

Their fragrance is fugitive, her handbook says, best
kept under cover of glass. And she loves
that what quickens within her then

is just sound and illusion, caught up
in wordplay's sudden wind, as a *fugitive scent*
slips past her, sloughs off its chains, high-steps

through sand scrub and the blackening night.
Not *memory*, not *tomorrow*, standing now in the bay bush.
Just a brush-stroke of fugitive *present*,

both held and released by the branches.

Overleaf:
William Merritt Chase, *The Bayberry Bush,* c. 1895.
Oil on canvas, 25 x 33 1/8 inches. The Parrish Art Museum,
Littlejohn Collection.

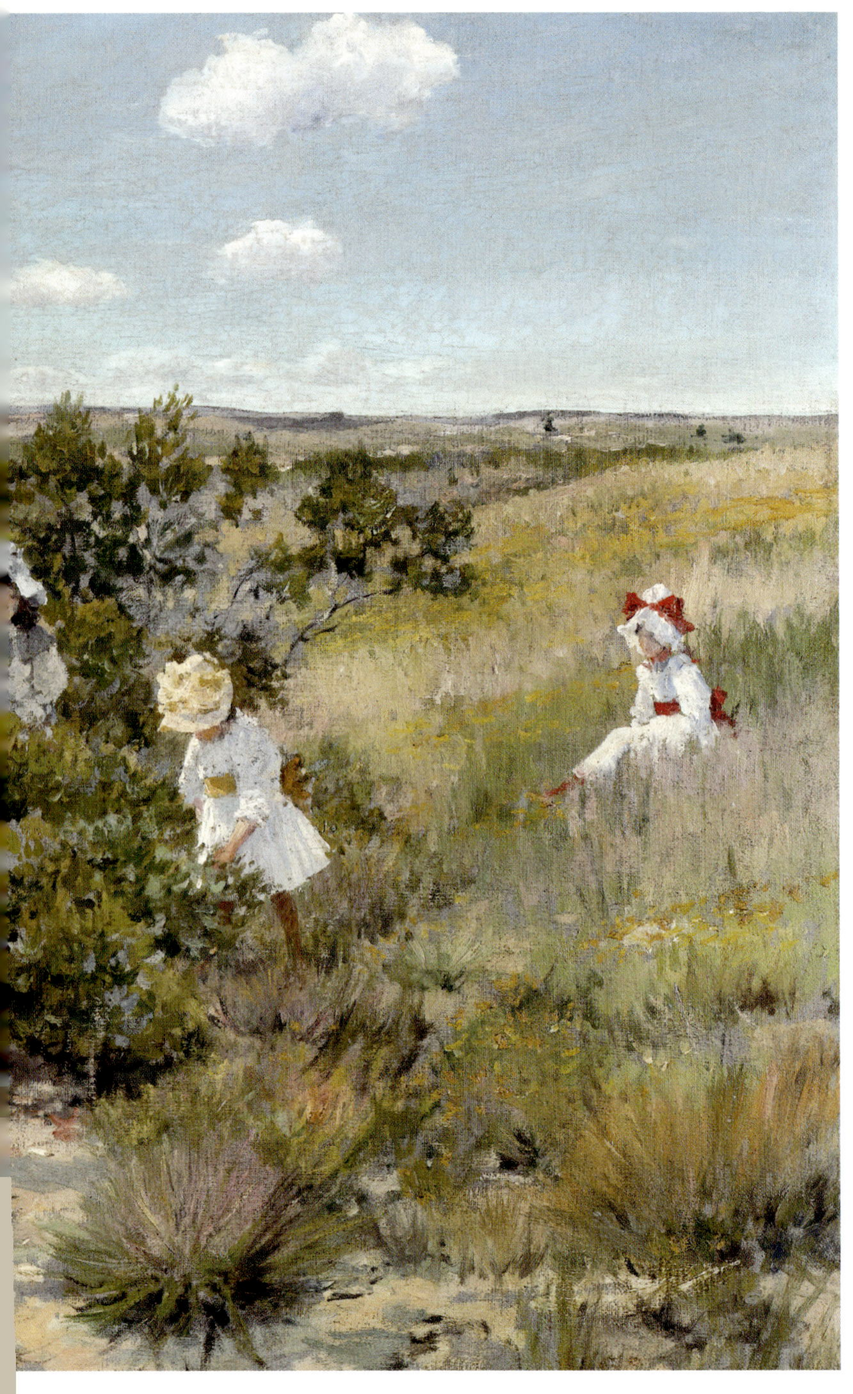

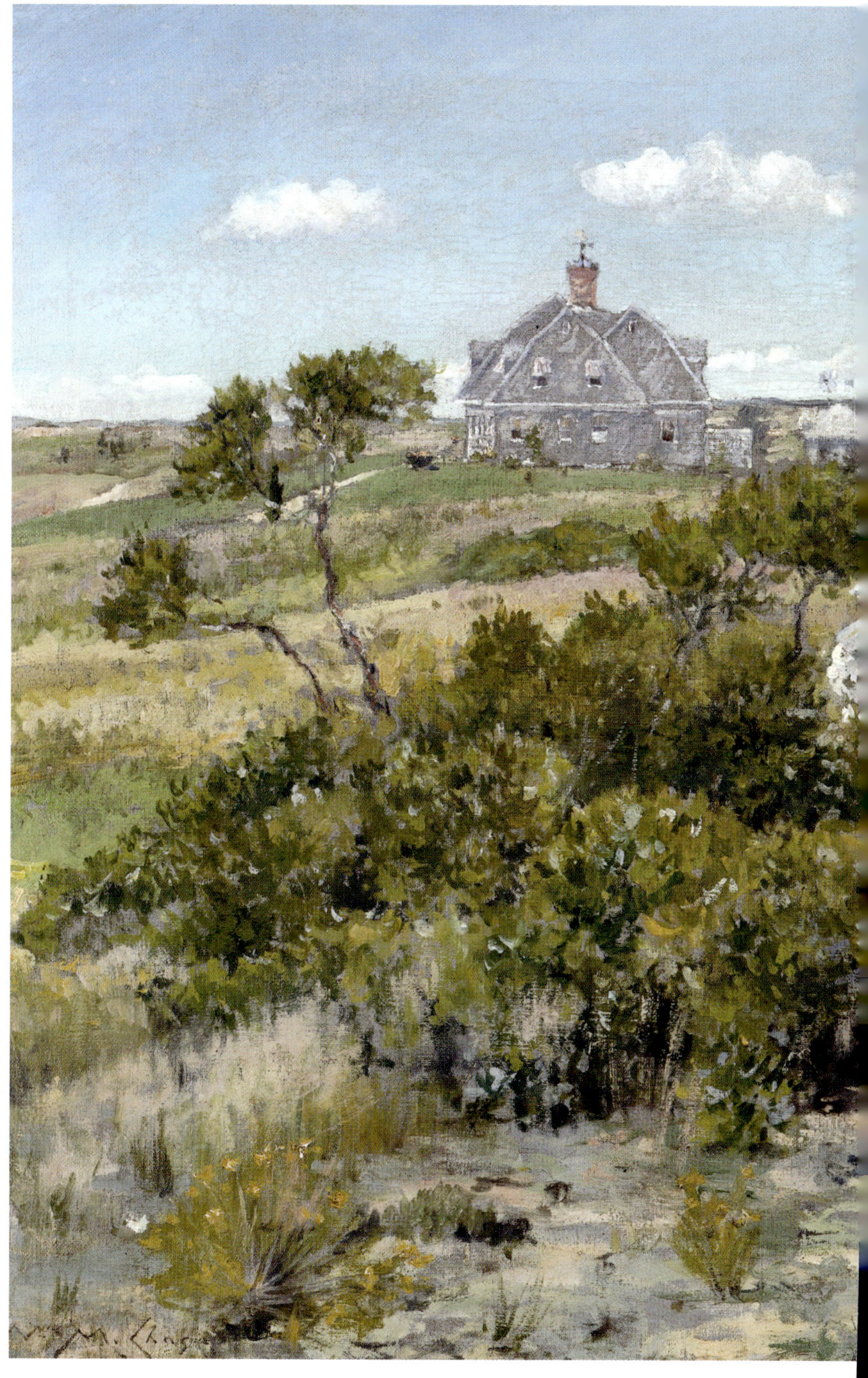

ALL AROUND *The Bayberry Bush*

SARAH BURNS

THE BAYBERRY BUSH OCCUPIES a prominent place in a suite of paintings revolving around William Merritt Chase's domestic life during the summers he spent in the Shinnecock Hills of Long Island. After his family first moved there, in 1892, Chase returned again and again to the theme of his wife and young daughters, sometimes together, sometimes apart, reading, lounging, or wandering in the scrubby sand hills surrounding the commodious Shingle Style cottage designed by the artist's friend Stanford White. In these paintings, the weather is almost always brilliant, the air clear, and the sky a deep or delicate blue, upholstered with perfect fluffy clouds. Arrayed in crisp white with colorful hats and sashes, the figures dot the landscape, each one a point of concentration for the highest, brightest values in the picture. The mood, invariably, is as sunny as the summer day.

The paintings vary in size. Some are informal oil sketches on board, and correspondingly small and intimate. Others, like the Parrish's painting, are on a considerably larger scale, which testifies to their status as important and ambitious productions. All the works testify to the artist's inveterate custom of painting *en plein air*, a practice he instilled in students who came to study under him at the Shinnecock Summer School of Art, established in 1891. The school was the pretext for the Chase family's annual seasonal migration. Their house was a realm apart, located a good three miles from the "Art Village," the center of instruction and social activities. At the Village, Chase expended large amounts

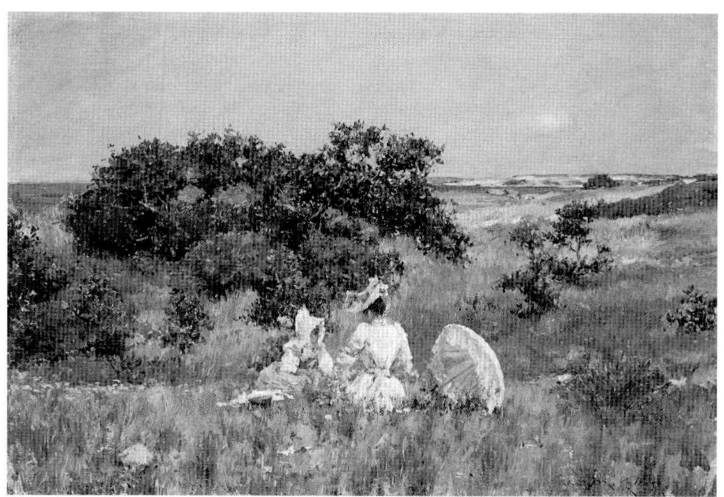

William Merritt Chase, *The Fairy Tale*, 1892. Oil on canvas, 16 x 24 inches. Collection of Margaret and Raymond Horowitz.

of professional energy as a dedicated and demanding instructor. He poured out his creative energies, however, in the immediate vicinity of the sturdy silvery-gray house that dominates the level horizon in *The Bayberry Bush*. We can gauge his attachment to the place by looking at *The Fairy Tale*, in which Mrs. Chase, in white, with a pink parasol, entertains one of her daughters. Commanding the scene is the very same bayberry bush from the other side, in the distance the blue waters of Peconic Bay. Chase had only to orbit the shrubbery to find another picture.

These are paintings in which very little is happening, beyond the experience of vacation pleasure. Even the activities, such as they are, seem desultory, as the title of *Idle Hours* (c. 1894; Amon Carter Museum, Fort Worth) makes abundantly clear. The pictures look so transparent, so sunny and serene, that one might think they pose few questions for the art historian. Since the revival of American Impressionism began roughly three decades ago, Chase's paintings made in the Shinnecock Hills and his situation there have been the subject of much scholarly attention. Ronald Pisano and others have detailed the story of the summer school, its patrons, and its students; described the house, the family, and the environment; and provided a solid context for understanding how Chase came to paint *The Bayberry Bush* and its pictorial siblings.[1] What questions, then, remain for the curious art historian to puzzle out, with respect above all to the Parrish painting?

The Bayberry Bush invites further scrutiny on a number of levels. First, a rereading of its formal properties reveals a more complex structure of relationships than might initially appear. These relationships, in turn, act as metaphors for natural, cultural, and familial connections. Second, we can examine the painting as evidence of work and inquire what kind of work (beyond the mere fact of making it) the artist performed in creating the picture. Third, we can view *The Bayberry Bush* as a sign of the artist himself, each of his marks a token of his presence and his actions in bringing this summer world into being.

More so than any of the other Shinnecock Hills landscapes, *The Bayberry Bush* undertakes a thorough inventory of the Chase family's domestic environment. In the foreground are three daughters, all in starchy white dresses with colorful trimmings. On the far right, Dorothy Brémond (b. 1891) sits in the spiky grass, her stockings, sash, and bonnet ribbons a vivid scarlet. A few feet below and closer to the middle, Helen Velasquez (b. 1895), in white and yellow, bends intently to the task of berry plucking. The eldest, Alice Dieudonnée, or Cosy (b. 1887), stands upright squarely on the center axis of the picture plane, full face to the viewer, and outfitted with touches of lavender blue. The branches of the bayberry bush screen her from the waist down.

Helen's appearance in the painting suggests that Chase could not have made this image earlier than 1897, when she would have been about two years old. If the work dates closer to 1895, then the youngest figure would have to be Hazel Neamaug, born in 1893. Since Hazel is seldom present in either Chase family photographs or her father's paintings, chances are that this is her younger, and presumably more patient or paintable, sister. Furthermore, in about 1897, Cosy's hair was cut in a style much like the one she sports in *The Bayberry Bush*.[2]

Behind Cosy is the family compound, the pump house surmounted by a weathervane almost directly above her head, and the angular masses of the house pinned together by a bulky central chimney the color of lobster bisque. Even though every feature of the house and grounds dissolves into a spot of color at close range, the level of description is high. We can see the cheerful red-and-white awnings shading several windows on the east and south sides, facing forward and to the left, respectively. We can count the columns on the roomy porch and see how velvety-green the lawn is, in contrast to the scraggly vegetation and gritty patches of sand beyond its perimeter. We can even make out the huge black iron cauldron, relic of Long Island's whaling industry, to the left of the porch, serving as a planter, full of bright orange blossoms. Flowering shrubs are planted close by the foundation, and a neat walkway runs parallel to the porch but breaks off when it reaches the edge of the yard.

In the foreground, clumps of beach grass decorate the pale, blue-shadowed sand. The rich green bayberry bush is all-encompassing, thrusting its branches high and wide in every direction and contrasting vibrantly with the bleached tints of the dunes. Above the scene, the sky is a diaphanous blue accented by serenely floating clouds as white as the girls' frocks.

The dynamic of *The Bayberry Bush* centers around a dialogue and intermingling of nature and culture. The house, of course, stands as a monument to culture's transformative powers. Its vivid green lawn—a domestic oasis—could not exist without sod, fertilizer, and liberal applications of water, brought up from far below by the mechanical toil of the pump. Unlike the gnarled, sprawling bayberry bush, the house shrubs are tidy and confined. Offsetting the expansive, open dunescape, Stanford White's handsome structure embodies the coalescent values of order and balance, art and craft. With its skin of shingles weathered silver, the house is at the same time subject to processes of organic change that link it symbolically with the surrounding natural environment.

The dunescape itself is liminal territory, a strip of dry, rugged wilderness fronting the shores of Shinnecock Bay on one side and Peconic Bay on the other. Yet here are three little girls, immaculate in their stiff ruffles and crisp bows, scattered incongruously among the rough, inhospitable vegetation. Emissaries from the oasis of order and culture behind them, they explore alien terrain. An invisible tether keeps them from roaming too far. Cosy, in the center, holds the clue to this tie that binds home and children. The axis around which everything else turns, Cosy is a visual rhyme or echo of the house behind her. The ruffled pyramid of her hat is repeated by the roofline of the pump house, which echoes the larger geometries of the house gables, stacked triangles gently broken by the double pitch of the gambrel roof. The massive chimney, suggesting interior warmth and comfort, stands in the precise center of the structure, just as Cosy stands in alignment with the exact midpoint of the composition. House and girl echo back and forth also in the colors they share: gray, gray-blue, and lavender.

Cosy was Chase's first-born, and from her earliest days a favorite model, appearing more frequently in his paintings than any of the other children. When asked why he privileged his eldest, Chase mused, "Why, I don't know. She very much resembles her mother."[3] Father's pet, mirror image and namesake of her mother, Cosy inhabits the landscape as surrogate for the maternal presence symbolized by the house on the horizon. Although Chase always claimed the role of family tastemaker and decorator, his devoted wife, Alice, his junior by seventeen years, made homes of the many houses the ever-growing family occupied over several decades, attending to countless practical details and supervising all domestic arrangements. Cosy, dead center, brings her mother's stability and calm into the untamed scrub where she has ventured with her younger sisters. Implied diagonals connect these two with Cosy and the home in the distance. The red-ribboned girl is the most potentially disorderly of the three. Off to the side by herself, touched with those bright scarlet accents, she is wayward and almost discordant. But the visual weight of her two sisters, lined up on the diagonal leading straight back to the house, effectively keeps her in balance. At least for now, nature and culture are in equilibrium, although the girls, tourists on excursion into the low-key wilderness of a seaside landscape, will in the end be drawn back into the sphere of home and mother.

Meanwhile, what of father? He is outside the scene, the legs of his easel and camp stool pushed down into the sand. Probably he is sheltering from the sun under the canopy of that outdoor painter's hallmark, the white umbrella. He is in his home precinct, three miles from the Art Village, yet is hard at work, fabricating this scene. Like any painting, *The Bayberry Bush* is the material evidence of the painter's labors. But beyond that, what is the nature of the work he has performed here?

In this and the other Shinnecock landscapes, Chase undertook a sustained demonstration of the art of seeing, and the painter's unique ability to see something where untutored (and untalented) eyes were utterly unable to detect aesthetic value. As a cosmopolitan, self-consciously professional, modern American artist, Chase had made a reputation for himself based on the acuity and refinement of his vision, and his unparalleled ability to translate visual sensation into paint. Although well trained in Europe, he cultivated the impression that what he did was natural, so much so that colleagues and critics described him as a "seeing machine" and "wonderful human camera" of great technical power.[4] But there was more to it than that. The journalist John Gilmer Speed visited Shinnecock in 1892 to prepare a report on Chase and his summer school. This, the first important publication on the school, gives an invaluable glimpse into life at Shinnecock.

Speed noted that for an artist, the sandy hills, the bays, and the ocean shore were repositories of pictures, so vast that an artist could set his easel up anywhere and be sure of a delightful, and paintable, view. "Prosaic eyes," it almost went without saying, could not see these pictures, but such eyes were "only half open anyway." Country people in the neighborhood, indeed, could never understand all the sketching in a landscape they considered unlovely, since the hills were neither fertile nor easy to negotiate. Having no practical or profitable use, they were considered absolutely worthless. For the painter, though, these sandy wastelands were visual treasure troves. In a half-hour's walk, Chase could see "enough of beauty to keep ten men busy for fifty years," whereas over the course of fifty years any given local would more than likely see a grand total of nothing.[5]

Discovering, seeing, and artistically recording this hidden beauty was the painter's way of adding value to the landscape, endowing it with aesthetic currency and redeeming it from its purported uselessness. It was now good for something, as source of refined visual pleasure for the cultured urbanites who had recently begun to build vacation homes in the Hamptons. These summer colonists had already driven up land values by turning shoreline properties into real estate. As more and more sought to purchase lots in the newly fashionable retreat, prices rose, from $2.50 an acre to $250.[6] The aesthetic value that Chase conferred on the landscape supplemented (and sublimated) its cash value, while it ratified the judgment and taste of new owners.

In addition, this land was of greatest utility as a huge outdoor classroom for the aspiring painters who flocked there in the summer to study with Chase. The students did most of their work in the open, once a week traveling as a group to a selected site and sketching there under Chase's supervision. One student painter,

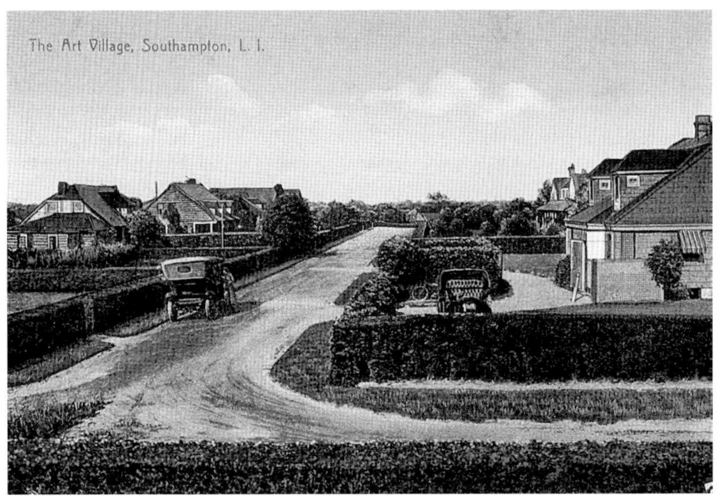

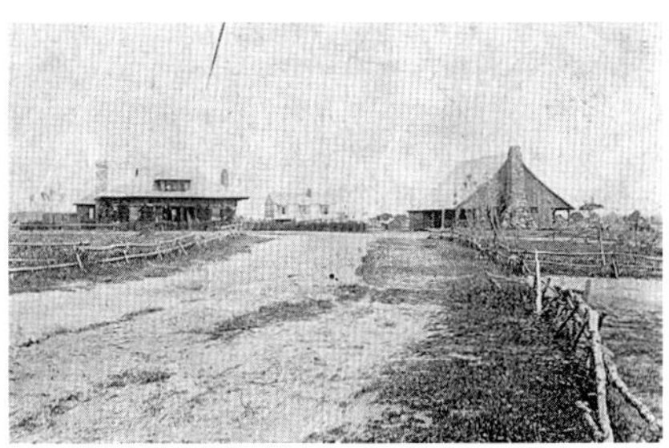

Postcard of the Art Village, c. 1891. Collection Eric Woodward.

View of the Art Village, c. 1900. Collection Southampton Historical Museum.

Rosina Emmet, recalled the look of the hills, dotted with easels, and described the school's purpose, to "teach the scholar to portray the outer world in the strong, vivid lights, which dazzle us on brilliant Summer days." An artist planting his easel in front of the dunes on a clear morning, she noted, looked at the "beautiful rainbow tints" of the vegetation with a mixture of delight and despair. To get such colors accurately, he could not fill his brush "with mauves too deep or yellows too brilliant."[7]

Chase's *Bayberry Bush* is the master's demonstration of how to carry out the goal of transcribing those "beautiful rainbow tints" with professional panache. He told his pupils that they must acquire a new set of colors for painting in the open air. They would need many more blues and greens, as many as they could possibly find. "When I go to my color merchant I tell him to show me all the blues and greens he has. There are skies that cannot be made with a permanent blue. There is an egg-shell blue that is the most difficult thing in the world to make. Magenta is a color you will find useful and difficult to make—get that." They must set their palettes with "every variety of color from white to black," arranging the different shades of blue and green from light to dark, the same way every day, until they could match visual sensation to color without even glancing to make sure they were swirling their brushes in the right puddle of paint.[8]

The Bayberry Bush shows us this palette in action. True to Chase's teaching, the canvas is a mosaic dominated by blues and greens in a complex variety of shades: slate blue, robin's-egg blue, lavender blue, greenish blue, azure, blues mingling with pea green; jade green, yellow-green, emerald green, and sage. Warm dabs and splashes of orange, pink, mauve, and red complement the cooler hues, and there are sparing touches of black and the dazzling white strokes reserved for patches of sunlit fabric. Each particle of paint is a record of the painter's time, energy, sensation, and expertise, applied to the process of transmuting raw material into work of art.

Even though we cannot see the painter himself, the painting is in every respect his stand-in, the sign of his presence and of his artistic identity. In the early years of his career in New York City, Chase filled his vast rooms in the Tenth Street Studio Building with a wealth of art and artifact meant to express his own taste and personality. Over the years, the studio served as both setting and subject for paintings that were also explicit or implicit self-portraits.[9] Chase set his mark as well on the landscapes he began to produce in his middle years. The painter in the landscape, obviously, could not hang drapes or fine-tune the arrangement of furniture. Yet he could make it equally the product and symbol of refined aesthetic

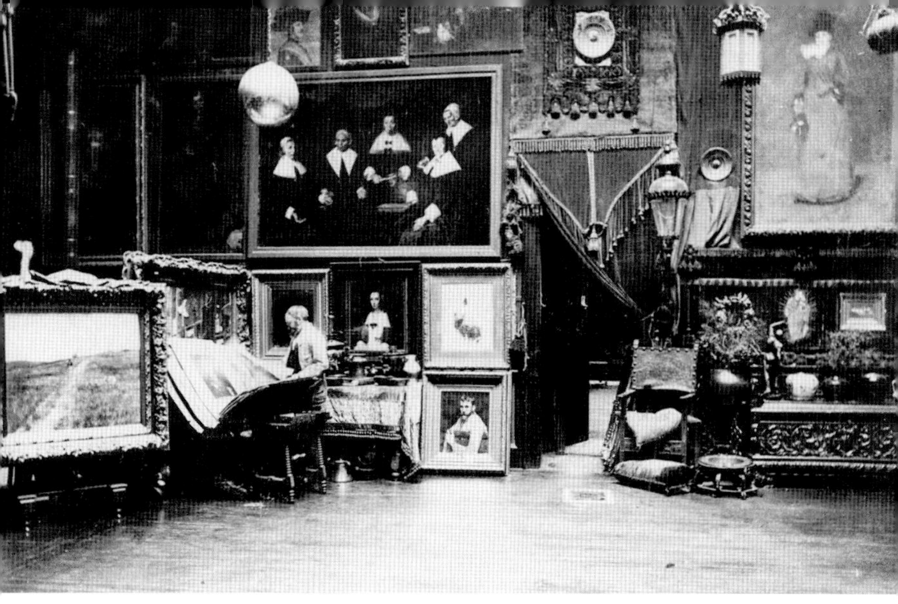

Chase in his Tenth Street studio, New York, surrounded by copies after Hals, Velázquez, and other Old Masters, c. 1895. Albumen print, 4½ x 7⅝ inches. The William Merritt Chase Archives, The Parrish Art Museum, Gift of Jackson Chase Storm.

sensibility, of a hand and an eye that could turn base landscape matter into pictorial gold.

The best way to appreciate this dimension of Chase's territory is to consider the degree of aesthetic control he brought into every area of his life. As mentioned, he was the stagemaster of decoration in both home and studio. It went even further than that. According to a writer who interviewed him for *The House Beautiful* magazine, Chase always insisted that "his wife and a long line of handsome children should wear artistic costumes."[10] Whether or not they did so in real life is difficult to say, but certainly it was true in art. While on his last trip to Spain, Chase wrote to his daughter Dorothy, "You must get ready to do a lot of posing for me when I get home. I have brought a lot of things which I know you will look nice in."[11] When *The Bayberry Bush* was painted, perhaps Cosy, Helen, and Dorothy just happened to wear those white dresses with the blue, yellow, and red accents; or perhaps their father intervened as stylist. Whatever the case, the artist also "dressed" the Shinnecock

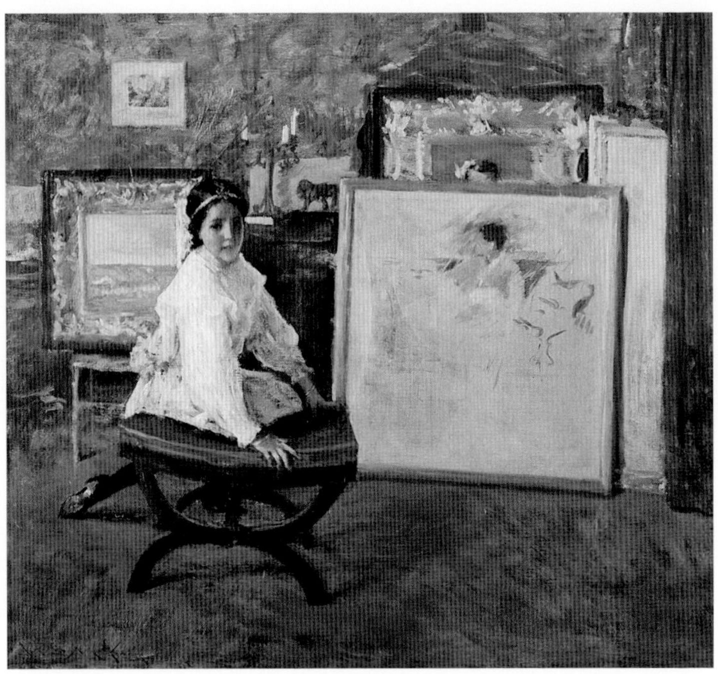

William Merritt Chase, *Did You Speak to Me?*, c. 1897. Oil on canvas, 38 x 43 inches. The Butler Institute of American Art, Youngstown, Ohio.

landscape, selecting the vantage point, posing the girls, and decking out the scene in a bright array of shimmering summery colors. In a literal sense he brought this pleasant world into being, fashioning the landscape to his own standards of harmony, taste, and beauty.

The Shinnecock landscape belonged to Chase in more ways than one. Like the objets d'art in his urban studio, this place was aesthetic property as well as real estate. Once painted, it became a precious, portable souvenir. The act of framing any given landscape was of particular significance. Performing the same function as a fence around some inviting tract, the frame staked Chase's claim to the beauties of an environment that only his eyes had been able to discover and reveal. Once framed, the landscape became studio decor among all the other furnishings that Chase continued to recycle into paintings. In *Did You Speak to Me?* a Shinnecock landscape in a heavy gold frame rests on a chair at left in the studio interior. On a stool in front of this painting is Cosy, in white with yellow sash and black stockings. She has apparently been gazing at the landscape brought into being by her father, but momentarily interrupted, she turns around and faces us. One of Chase's lovely studio furnishings, she might have just walked out of the painted dunes in the picture behind her. On the other side, a partially completed portrait (perhaps of Cosy once more, or of her mother) leans against yet another painting of a daughter with a floppy bow in her hair.

Did You Speak to Me? represents a complex fusion of art with family, landscape, and the material world, all of them grist for Chase's aesthetic mill. The same kind of fusion has taken place in *The Bayberry Bush*. The painter transformed the environs of his summer home into an open-air studio, each tuft of heather, each colorful bow, each puffy cloud pressed into service as artistic prop or property. Famous for that camera vision, Chase convinces us that this was a faithful transcription of the scene before his eyes. At the same time, he made over all the elements—house, girls, sand, and that vigorous, monumental bush—into the perfected vision of a perfect and never-ending summer day. Today, *The Bayberry Bush* allows us to behold this lost world once again, through the eyes of its premier artist-patriarch.

NOTES

1. The most extensive study of Chase's Shinnecock landscapes is D. Scott Atkinson and Nicolai Cikovsky, Jr., *William Merritt Chase: Summers at Shinnecock, 1891–1902* (Washington, DC: National Gallery of Art, 1987). Also see Ronald G. Pisano, *Long Island Landscape Painting 1820–1920* (Boston: Little, Brown, 1985), pp. 112–121, and *A Leading Spirit in American Art: William Merritt Chase, 1849–1916* (Seattle: Henry Art Gallery Association, University of Washington, 1983). Also useful is Keith L. Bryant, Jr., *William Merritt Chase: A Genteel Bohemian* (Columbia: University of Missouri Press, 1991), pp. 141–182. Still indispensable is the important early biography by Chase's former student Katherine Metcalf Roof, *The Life and Art of William Merritt Chase* (1917; repr. New York: Hacker Art Books, 1975). William H. Gerdts, "The Teaching of Painting Out-of-Doors in America in the Late Nineteenth Century," in Bruce Weber and William H. Gerdts, *Nature's Ways: American Landscape Painting of the Late Nineteenth Century* (West Palm Beach, FL: Norton Gallery of Art, 1987), pp. 25–40, is a valuable history and analysis of the summer schools, their emergence and influence.
2. See her photograph from c. 1897 in Ronald G. Pisano and Alicia Grant Longwell, *Photographs from the William Merritt Chase Archives at The Parrish Art Museum* (Southampton, NY: The Parrish Art Museum, 1992), fig. 68, p. 33. Roof, p. 273, observes that Cosy posed probably more often than any other painter's child in America, with Dorothy a close second.
3. Bryant, p. 107.
4. Kenyon Cox, "William Merritt Chase, Painter," *Harper's New Monthly Magazine*, 78 (March 1889), p. 549.
5. John Gilmer Speed, "An Artist's Summer Vacation," *Harper's New Monthly Magazine*, 87 (June 1893), pp. 3–14.
6. Ibid., p. 9.
7. Rosina H. Emmet, "The Shinnecock Art School," *The Art Interchange*, 31 (October 1893), pp. 89–90.
8. Chase, "Out-of-Door Sketching," *The Art Interchange*, 39 (July 1897), p. 8.
9. See Sarah Burns, "The Price of Beauty: Art, Commerce, and the Late Nineteenth-Century American Studio Interior," in David Miller, ed., *American Iconology* (New Haven, CT: Yale University Press, 1993), pp. 209–238.
10. James William Pattison, "William Merritt Chase, NA," *The House Beautiful*, 25 (February 1909), p. 52.
11. Roof, p. 221.

WILLIAM MERRITT CHASE'S *The Bayberry Bush:*

TABLEAUX VIVANTS, NATURE MORTE, AND THE SUMMER OF 1895

ALICIA GRANT LONGWELL

> *William B.* [sic] *Chase, President of the Society of American Artists, thought the bronze statues were modest in the extreme, and did not consider the exhibition of copies of paintings on a public stage more immodest than the exhibition of originals in a public art gallery.*
>
> *"Do you not consider such an exhibition injurious to public morals?" asked Justice Sims.*
>
> *"No, Sir," replied Chase. "I would gladly take my wife and daughters to see the statues."*[1]

Of all the arbiters of public taste in the New York of 1895, it is significant that William Merritt Chase was the one summoned to testify on the probity of certain *tableau vivant* performances in the city. A practice in which costumed participants in their dress and attitude replicate Old Master paintings, *tableaux vivants* were popularized in the United States in the 1850s as a fashionable parlor game and by the 1890s had become an indispensable feature of Gilded Age society "at-homes" and charity balls. Chase's renown in staging such events would have made him the artist most likely to be called as a witness for the defense.

The theatrical troupe in question had caused a sensation during its performance by using almost nude male models, who were covered with a bronze powder to give them the illusion of statuary. What landed members of the company in jail, however, was the introduction of several female models clad in the same manner. Chase's response to the furor points to his belief in the seamlessness of art and everyday life. The sensibilities of his wife and daughters were the touchstone for his opinion.

Later that same year, 1895, we find Chase, his wife, and their family once more installed in their summer home in the Shinnecock Hills, near Southampton, New York, where Chase had begun his fifth year teaching at the Shinnecock Summer School of Art. Typically, Chase ventured into Southampton Village only on Mondays, when critiques of student work were conducted at the studio building in the "Art Village," a cluster of houses where students lived and worked. On Tuesdays, he gave instruction *en plein air* wherever students set up their easels. The rest of the week was reserved for his own painting and for time with his family. In New York City, Chase's day was clearly divided between home and studio—the latter in the Tenth Street Studio Building, in splendid rooms filled with exotic tapestries, ceramics, and assorted bric-a-brac that vied for attention with the Old Master paintings lining the walls. At Shinnecock, his studio was in a room converted for that purpose on the northwest side of the family home, which was designed by Stanford White. The demarcation between artistic practice and family life was less distinct in the Shinnecock Hills, and Chase employed his wife and daughters as models, to the exclusion of almost all others, during summers there.

In *The Bayberry Bush,* three of the artist's daughters are dispersed in the sparse landscape of the Hills. The frontality and steadfast gaze of Alice Dieudonnée, the eldest, differs noticeably from the poses of her sisters, who have been permitted to become absorbed in their own activities. Is Alice responding to a cue from her father, while the other two have been directed to "go on with your play"? Might her central position in this plein-air stage set allude to a *tableau vivant*? As naturally as Chase borrowed from the Old Masters, he reinvented these stagings for his own life in art.

Tableaux vivants *depend for their effect not only on the happy disposal of lights and the delusive interposition of layers of gauze, but on a corresponding adjustment of the mental vision. To unfurnished minds they remain, in spite of every enhancement of art, only a superior kind of wax-works; but to the responsive fancy they may give magic glimpses of the boundary world between fact and imagination.*

This is how Edith Wharton, in her novel of turn-of-the-century New York manners *The House of Mirth,* describes an evening at the Wellington Brys', where a series of *tableaux vivants* was the evening's chief entertainment. Chase may well have been Wharton's model for the "distinguished portrait-painter" Paul Morpeth, whose stagings assured the society hostess of a successful evening. Those "magic glimpses" to which Wharton refers enable the hero, Lawrence Selden, to indulge his fantasies fully while observing the novel's hapless heroine, Lily Bart, in a pose borrowed from Sir Joshua Reynolds's painting *Mrs. Lloyd*. The assembled guests might have viewed this embodiment of Reynolds's depiction of a young betrothed woman writing her future name on a tree trunk as a charming vignette, but the tableau would have had more specific meaning for Lily, whose marriageability was a constant concern to her. She might well have negotiated with the *metteur-en-scène* (the Chase figure) for the privilege of playing this role, knowing that Selden, among other eligible bachelors in the audience, would take advantage of the opportunity to gaze openly at her silent and immobile form.

What were Chase's links with *tableaux vivants*? Such parlor theatricals were probably not part of his childhood in rural Indiana, near the town of Ninevah, where his mother helped organize the Methodist congregation in 1853.[2] By that time there were scores of *tableau vivant* handbooks in print, including W. Frikell's *Parlor Theatricals; or Winter Evenings' Entertainment* (1859), in which elaborate instructions were accompanied by reassurances to the reader that the "tinseled fascination of the stage may be mimicked at the home fireside."[3] Manuals described how to create a stage in the parlor, position uprights to indicate a frame, and drape black curtains most effectively to achieve a shallow space for the sitter. When the Chase family left the puritanical sphere of the countryside and moved to the state capital, Indianapolis, in 1861, young Merritt would have had the opportunity to visit theaters where touring opera companies and others performed. But it was only after he went to study at the academy in Munich in 1872 that he started to indulge his penchant for reproducing the poses of Old Master paintings, particularly the Dutch school. Costume balls and masquerades were established rituals in Munich art circles; the tradition dated back to the religious and civic pageants of medieval Europe. An early biographer of the artist writes that his fellow student Frank Duveneck recalled "the interesting effects Chase contrived in his studio by posing a model in a frame in the semblance of some famous canvas of the great masters. Those were his first experiments in the old-master tableaux with which he afterwards familiarized New York."[4]

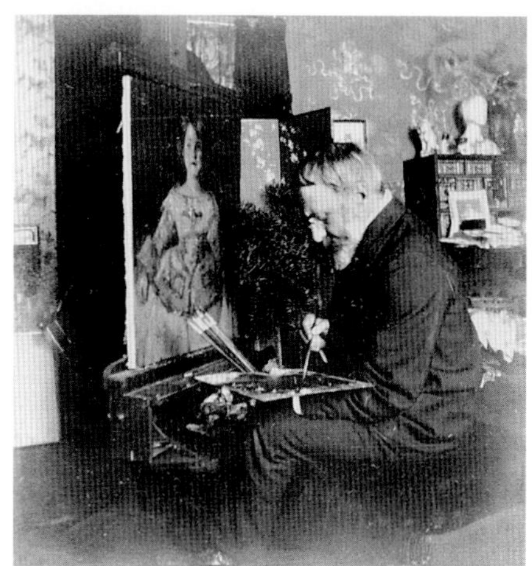

Chase painting a portrait of Helen as an infanta of Velázquez, c. 1899. Gelatin printing-out paper, 3 x 3 3/8 inches. The William Merritt Chase Archives, The Parrish Art Museum, Gift of Mrs. A. Byrd McDowell.

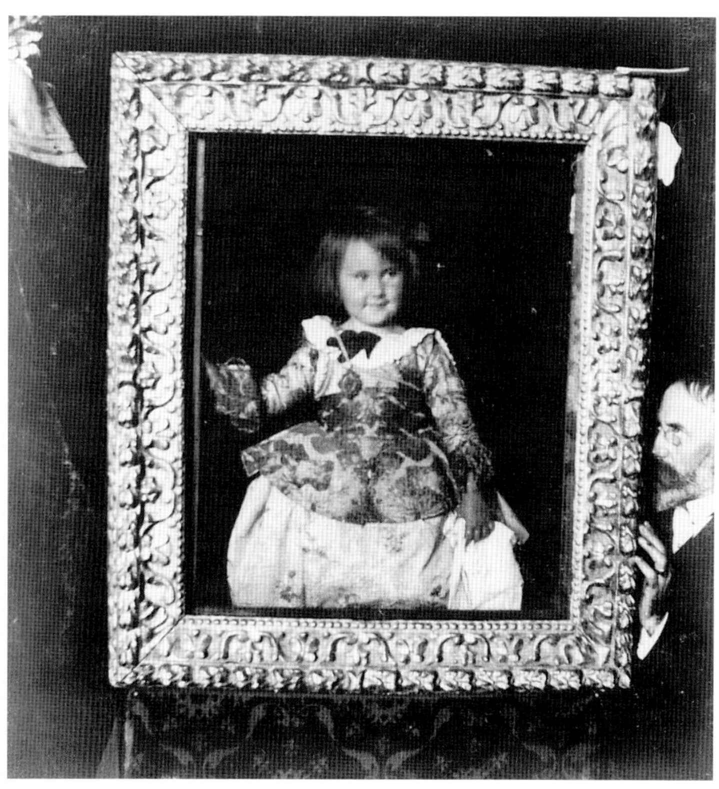

Chase adjusting the *tableau vivant* frame behind which Helen poses as an infanta, c. 1899. Gelatin printing-out paper, 3 x 3 inches. The William Merritt Chase Archives, The Parrish Art Museum, Gift of Mrs. A. Byrd McDowell.

Soon after returning to New York from his studies abroad, Chase was introduced by a friend, the artist Frederick S. Church, to the Gerson family. The three daughters, Virginia, Minnie, and Alice (whom Chase would marry in 1887), became muses and models for him, and evenings at the Gerson home were often spent making silhouettes, fashioning fantastic pictures on sheets of paper covered with the young men's cigar ash, and staging parlor theatricals. In a memoir, the daughter of C. H. Joaquin Miller, a poet who frequented the Gerson salon, described an evening in which "the beautiful

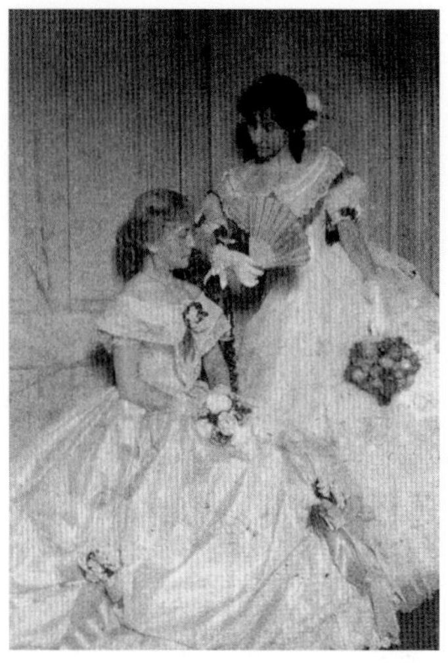

Minnie (left) and Virginia Gerson, sisters of Alice Gerson Chase, c. 1906. Gelatin silver print, 4 x 3 5/8 inches, mounted on board. The William Merritt Chase Archives, The Parrish Art Museum, Gift of Jackson Chase Storm.

Alice Gerson, engaged to William Merritt Chase, posed as an Indian Maiden, scanning the landscape for her lover."[5] A photograph by Gertrude Käsebier shows the two older sisters, Virginia and Minnie, in elaborate evening gowns for the Assembly Ball of 1906 (also known as the "Crinoline Ball," for the mid-nineteenth-century costumes traditionally worn.[6] The elder Gerson sisters, who never married, were evidently quite comfortable with the idea of dress-up—Minnie would have been fifty-three at the time of the photograph, and Virginia forty-two. Their pose as debutantes transgresses the boundaries of reality and enters a fantasy realm. Much like a *tableau vivant,* this costumed scene staged for Käsebier's camera hints that the sisters had an ongoing practice of constructing other selves—perhaps their way of managing a limited freedom within a social structure especially confining for unmarried females.

Historical antecedents of the *tableau vivant* can be found in medieval pageants and the subsequent fashion of Elizabethan masques. Classical French theater of the seventeenth century used the effect of the tableau to draw attention to key moments in the drama. Indeed, any drama that privileges the eye over the ear and uses melodrama to make emotion explicit can be directly linked to the *tableau vivant.* The first practitioner of what might be called the private, domestic-parlor aspect of the *tableau vivant* was the renowned beauty Emma Hart, the mistress and later the wife of Sir William Hamilton, British envoy to the Kingdom of the Two Sicilies

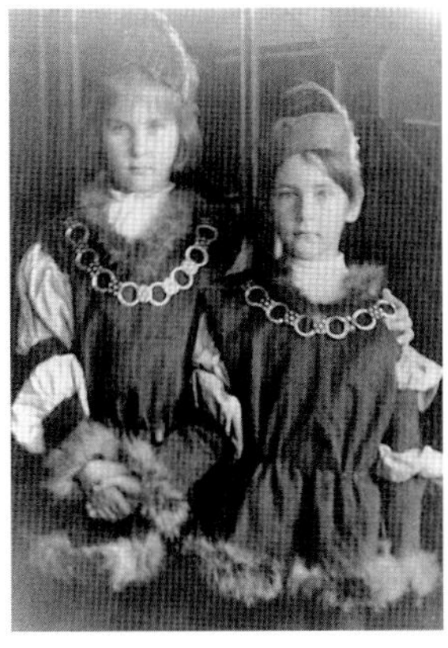

Helen and Robert Chase, c. 1903. Gelatin printing-out paper, 4 x 3 1/8 inches. The William Merritt Chase Archives, The Parrish Art Museum.

in the late 1700s. At his villa in Naples he built his own private art gallery, which included a large box lined with black cloth and surrounded by a gold frame. It was in this frame that Emma would assume her various "attitudes." With a minimum of props, but with the prodigious use of numerous cashmere shawls, she was able to transmute herself into multiple personae, much to the delight of Hamilton and his frequent guests, including Goethe, among other distinguished figures of the period. By all accounts her most moving interpretations were of women betrayed by their passions and wronged by their male protectors.

The first recorded public performances of *tableaux vivants* on the New York stage came during the theater season of 1831–1832, when the actress Ada Adams Barrymore portrayed "the beautiful Print of THE SOLDIER'S WIDOW," as an advertisement read. Subsequent performances included larger tableaux, such as the "Signing of the Declaration of Independence," with its fifty-six figures.[7] By the late 1840s, actresses were replaced by "model artists" in flesh-colored tights whose repertoire relied heavily on paintings of nudes. In 1847, the touring troupe led by a Dr. Collyer enjoyed an immediate success. The *New York Herald* critic effused:

> *We attended the first exhibition of Dr. Collyer's troupe of model artists last evening, and we are free to say that they excel anything of the kind we have ever seen in New York. . . . We saw accurate representations of the most exquisite works of the most renowned [artists] of the old world—such as Titian, Van dyke [*sic*], Rembrandt,*

and a host of others, equally celebrated: and we learned from persons present who have seen the originals, the personifications of the last evening were very accurate.[8]

During the 1870s and 1880s, as these productions grew more and more scandalous, they came under the scrutiny of the morals watchdog Anthony Comstock. It was the parallel development of the domestic aspect of the genre, the parlor theatrical and high-society performances of *tableaux vivants,* that made Chase the leading practitioner and, as we have seen, an expert witness.

Surviving programs from public stagings of *tableaux vivants* attest that Chase was much in demand as a director. Although many were produced as charitable benefits, Chase may have been remunerated for his participation. An 1890 program announced, among its "living pictures by American artists," renderings by Chase of Velázquez, Van Dyck, and Gainsborough. A program for a performance under Chase's direction for the benefit of the St. Katherine Home in Jersey City, to be held at Castle Point in Hoboken on May 9 (probably 1891, when Chase was living in Hoboken), lists "Portrait by Van Dyke; Mme. Recamier; Charlotte Corday; *Solitude* by Sir F. Leighton." One of the artist's last staged efforts was created in the year before his death; part of a benefit for the American Ambulance Hospital

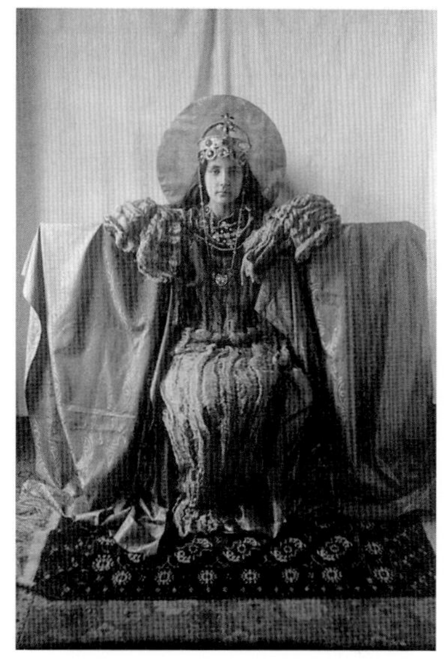

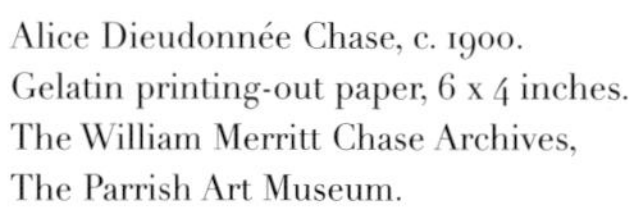

Alice Dieudonnée Chase, c. 1900. Gelatin printing-out paper, 6 x 4 inches. The William Merritt Chase Archives, The Parrish Art Museum.

in Paris, and held in the grand ballroom of New York's Ritz-Carlton Hotel in April 1915, it featured "living portraits after the Old Masters, posed by Mr. William M. Chase (assisted by Miss Elizabeth Fisher)."[9]

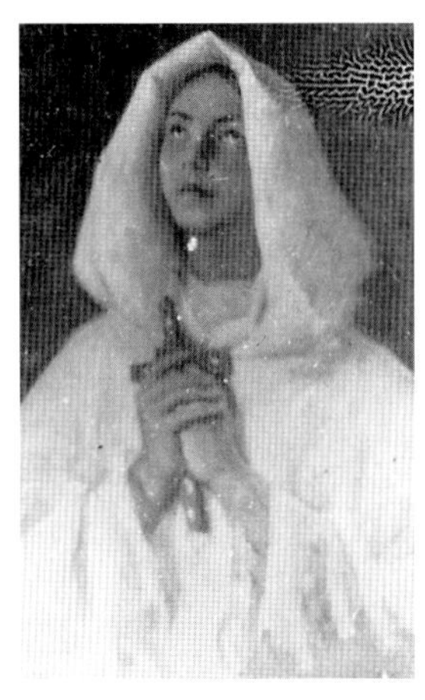

Chase's *Devotion*, a portrait of one of his daughters, c. 1898. Gelatin printing-out paper, 1 5/16 x 3/4 inches. The William Merritt Chase Archives, The Parrish Art Museum, Gift of Mrs. A. Byrd McDowell.

To judge from the large number of photographs in the Parrish's Chase Archives that show the artist's daughters posing in costume at Shinnecock, the staging of tableaux was a significant part of the summer activities at home and in the Art Village. So successful was his posing of his daughter Helen after a Velázquez infanta at an Art Village soirée that a Southampton summer resident, Mrs. Henry Kirke Porter, commissioned Chase to paint a picture of this very subject for her.[10] Other paintings depict the Chase daughters in costume poses, often taking as their subject vulnerable female characters from fairy tales and religious iconography, as seen in *Little Red Riding Hood* and *Devotion*.

In *The Bayberry Bush*, though, we see the girls not in elaborate costume but in simple summer play frocks. The artist's daughters are the most frequent inhabitants of the Shinnecock landscapes, the outdoor scenes Chase painted during the summers he taught on Long Island. (Between 1903 and 1913 he held the seasonal classes in Europe, and in 1914 he taught his last summer classes, in Carmel-by-the-Sea, California.) Chase almost always signed his paintings; he dated them with less frequency. Many works made at Shinnecock before or during the summer of 1892 can be dated accurately, because they were reproduced in an article by John Gilmer Speed published in the June 1893 edition of *Harper's New Monthly Magazine*, entitled "An Artist's Summer Vacation." The dating of subsequent paintings has been based largely on the presumed age of the Chase daughters and on various stylistic considerations.

Stylistically, the Shinnecock landscapes have a distinct evolution. This was first remarked on in an insightful essay by Nicolai Cikovsky, Jr., in the catalogue accompanying the 1987 exhibition *William Merritt Chase: Summers at Shinnecock*. Cikovsky suggests earlier and later periods for the Shinnecock paintings, and points out a definite stylistic shift in work done after 1895. He finds that Chase moves away from an "Impressionistic treatment," with "uncomplicated descriptiveness, with a savor of sensation and a pure pleasure in seeing and what is seen." In the early landscapes Cikovsky observes "an inescapable feeling of innocence." Paintings from the middle to late 1890s, he adds, are more aptly described as "expressive"—that is, less given to Impressionistic color, more likely to make use of intense diagonals in the composition, not as sunny in climate or mood, and less likely to depict the artist's family (see *The Pot Hunter,* page 43).[11]

The Bayberry Bush is plainly situated in the transitional period of 1895. We will not, in fact, see the treatment of the foreground and the figures "staged" in the landscape in quite the same way again in Chase's work.

Informative details about Chase's family have recently come to light from a Bible whose illuminated pages record dates of births and deaths. The birth date of the fifth Chase daughter, Helen Velasquez, is given as May 26, 1897, two years later than has been believed; this implies that the youngest daughter in *The Bayberry Bush* is Dorothy, born in 1891, or Hazel, born in 1893. Yet even more astonishing is the revelation of the birth of a son, John Rudolph, on August 16, 1894, and his death almost exactly a year later, on August 10, at Shinnecock, and the birth later that summer of twin girls, Mabel Claire and Sarah Virginia, on September 20, and their deaths at Shinnecock on September 20 and October 11, 1895, respectively.

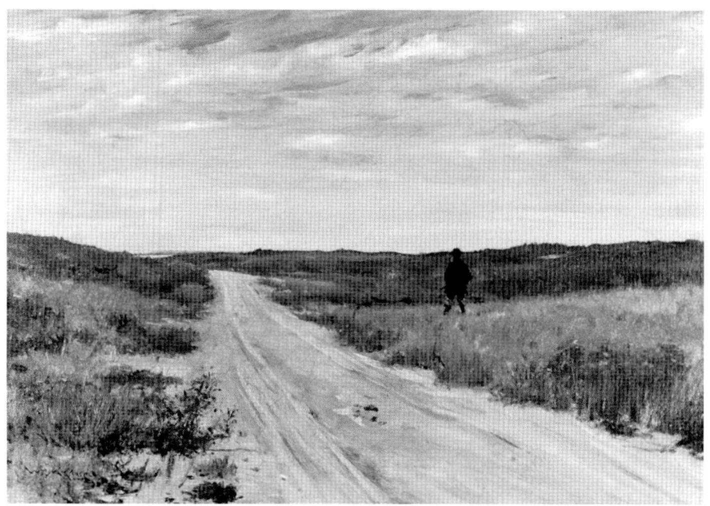

William Merritt Chase, *The Pot Hunter*, c. 1897. Oil on canvas, 16 1/4 x 24 1/8 inches. The Parrish Art Museum, Purchase Fund and Gift of Mr. Frank Sherer.

This would mean that the family stayed in the Shinnecock Hills well into October, and would explain the late-summer, early-fall vegetation in *The Bayberry Bush*—and establish the work as an elegiac coda to the first phase of the Shinnecock paintings. Dating the picture to 1895 would mean that Alice turned eight the year it was painted, and was two years older than her next-younger sibling—and old enough to have some understanding of what was happening in the family. The succession of radical changes after October 1895, when the second twin was buried, bespeaks a year of despair and disruption for the Chases. In what may have been an accommodation to the family's staying at Shinnecock past the start of autumn classes in New York City, Chase resigned his teaching positions at the school of the Brooklyn Art Association and the Art Students League that year. In January 1896 he gave up his space in the Tenth Street Studio Building, which had for the previous seventeen years been a showcase for the marketing of his art. He auctioned off the entire contents, including paintings and years' worth of other accumulated objects. At the end of that month, he sailed for Europe with Mrs. Chase, Alice Dieudonnée, and Dorothy, to hold classes in Madrid and to travel and teach for four months.

The artist and his family returned to Shinnecock in the summer of 1896, and in the autumn he founded the Chase School of Art in New York and began teaching at the Pennsylvania Academy of the Fine Arts in Philadelphia. Nonetheless, the previous year had by any reckoning been tumultuous, and the tragedy of the deaths of three infants in two months would explain the abrupt changes. Perhaps Chase contemplated abandoning the Shinnecock School after the devastating summer and devised the alternative plan to take classes to Europe. The fact that Mrs. Chase went with him might suggest that her mourning for the loss of the children had descended into melancholia; the trip may have been meant as a diversion and a tonic. Infant mortality was high at the time, but even in this period the expectancy of survival had increased. Three losses in such quick succession could have had only a profound effect on the entire family.

Chase's career as influential painter and teacher extended long after the summer of 1895 at Shinnecock, yet the year stands as a divide in both his art and his life. Three children were born after Helen in 1897: Robert Stewart in 1898, Roland Dana in 1901, and Mary Content in 1904, and Mrs. Chase and the children spent summers at Shinnecock even after Chase took to accompanying summer classes abroad in 1903. He would never recapture, in mood or execution, the transparency of the early Shinnecock paintings. His best-known works in the decade before his death in 1916 were still lifes of dead fish—bravura brushwork lavished on the depiction of inanimate life. The seamless unity of art and life conveyed in the paintings of his family—staged as carefully as *tableaux vivants*—is his enduring legacy.

NOTES

1. *The New York Times,* March 27, 1895, p. 8, cited in Jack McCullough, *Tableaux Vivants on the Nineteenth Century New York Stage* (Ann Arbor, MI: UMI Research, 1983), p. 38.
2. Keith L. Bryant, Jr., *William Merritt Chase: A Genteel Bohemian* (Columbia: University of Missouri Press, 1991), p. 2.
3. Karen Halttunen, *Confidence Men and Painted Women* (New Haven, CT: Yale University Press, 1982).
4. Katherine Metcalf Roof, *The Life and Art of William Merritt Chase* (1917; repr. New York: Hacker Art Books, 1975), p. 43.
5. Juanita J. Miller, *My Father, C. H. Joaquin Miller, Poet* (Oakland, CA: Tooley-Town, c. 1941), p. 88.
6. Judith Frayer Davidov, *Women's Camera Work: Self/Body/Other* (Durham, NC: Duke University Press, 1998), p. 64.
7. For these performances, see McCullough, pp. 15, 30.
8. *New York Herald,* September 24, 1847, cited ibid., p. 38.
9. For the 1890 and 1891 performances, see programs in the "Tableaux Vivants" clipping file at the New York Public Library for the Performing Arts. I am grateful to Katrina Mason for providing me with documentation of the 1915 staging.
10. Roof, p. 185.
11. D. Scott Atkinson and Nicolai Cikovsky, Jr., *William Merritt Chase: Summers at Shinnecock, 1891–1902* (Washington, DC: National Gallery of Art, 1987), pp. 33–34.

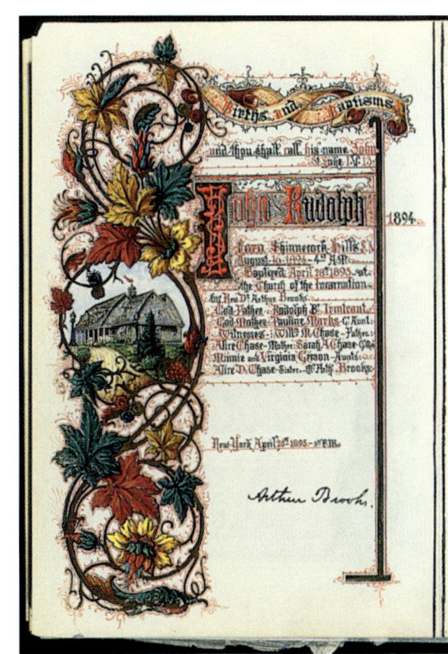

Page from a Chase family Bible, with illumination by Baron Rudolph B. Irmtraut, godfather to John Rudolph Chase.

ARTISTS' PROJECTS

Essays by Ingrid Schaffner and Melissa Feldman

RICHARD ARTSCHWAGER

KNUT ÅSDAM

CAI GUO-QIANG

BONNIE COLLURA

PETER DOIG

JOSEPH GRIGELY

JITKA HANZLOVÁ

JOAN JONAS

LEE MINGWEI

JOSÉ ALEJANDRO RESTREPO

BEVERLY SEMMES

YUTAKA SONE

RICHARD ARTSCHWAGER

Born in Washington, D.C., in 1923. Lives in Hudson, New York.

What is it to look? How does one ground that experience through works of art? Richard Artschwager has been pressing images from everyday life—tables, chairs, rooms, houses, buildings, landscapes, people—into the service of these questions since the 1960s. To mediate his exploration, Artschwager (who trained in science and music before turning to art) has made extensive use of photography. His fuzzy-looking black-and-white paintings are based directly on reproductions, mostly from newspapers. His sculptural material of choice is Formica, a plastic laminate that photographically captures the look of real wood or stone. Faux, trompe l'oeil, simulation—the tricks of the decorator's trade, not the conventions of fine art—give Artschwager's work its capacity to transmute banal subjects into disconcerting objects, which demand simply to be seen. (He has made a number of works over the years under the rubric of Expressionism/Impressionism, in which some abstract element always appears to push into or poke out of the picture frame.)

And so it came as a disappointment when Artschwager initially declined to participate in this exhibition, which is about looking at a picture, and an Impressionist one at that. Intrigued by photography, the French Impressionists too attempted to represent objectively phenomena of visual perception. William Merritt Chase considered such practices distracting, but he made good use of the movement's dappled brushwork and vibrant atmosphere when he painted *The Bayberry Bush*. It was Artschwager's respect for Chase's efforts that made him disinclined to participate. "It does the Here and Now (impressionism)," he commented. "I like being aware of the Hamptons from a distance." He pointed out the particular resonance between the girls' white dresses and the white clouds above. Perhaps wary that these qualities of Chase's work might become the subject of irony, Artschwager changed his mind.

The Bayberry Bush reminded Artschwager of his own painting *The Cloudy Day* (1994), and he started his project with relatively small reproductions of the two works. Proceeding digitally, he stretched and squeezed the copy of his until it matched the proportions of Chase's. He then subjected both reproductions to a process of enlargement—to "rot the picture quality"—until they reached the size of the nineteenth-century canvas. The resulting pictures were framed identically as computer-generated Iris prints. Observe: *The Cloudy Day* underwent its transformation with frame, *The Bayberry Bush* without. That's because Artschwager built his frame into the work; Chase's painting sits inside a modern addition, which, incidentally, is being replaced by a period frame in time for this exhibition.

Artschwager says he wants to drive "each of these two into a generic zone to the point where the distinction between the two pictures begins to become blurred, stirring up a kind of generic seeing (of pictures in general)." In other words, by exaggerating the Impressionist rot and modern pixels of mechanical reproduction, Artschwager tunes out any critical or historical distance to bring both his picture and Chase's into plain view. I.S.

Readings

Richard Armstrong, *Artschwager, Richard,* New York: Whitney Museum of American Art, 1988. Arthur Danto et al., *Richard Artschwager,* Paris: Fondation Cartier pour l'Art Contemporain, 1994. Suzanne Delehanty et al., *Richard Artschwager's Theme(s),* Philadelphia: Institute of Contemporary Art, University of Pennsylvania, 1979. David Frankel, "Curtain Call: The Art of Richard Artschwager," *Artforum,* November 2000. Ingrid Schaffner et al., "Richard Artschwager," *Parkett,* no. 47 (1996).

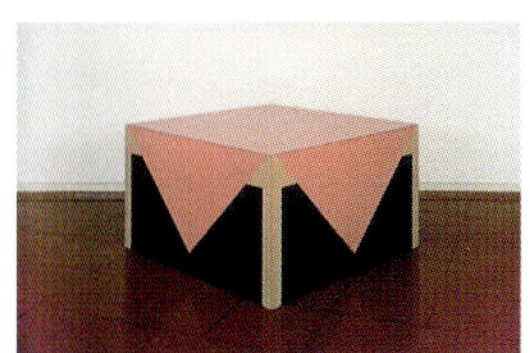

RICHARD ARTSCHWAGER, *Table with Pink Tablecloth,* 1964. Formica on wood, 25 x 44 x 44 inches.

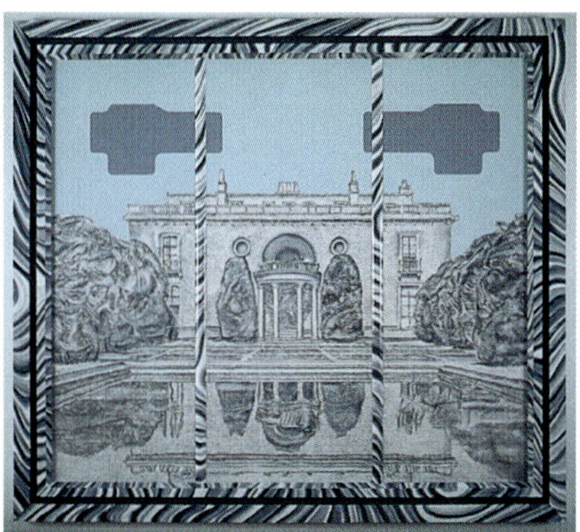

The Cloudy Day, 1994. Acrylic, Formica, Celotex, and wood, 68 x 78 inches.

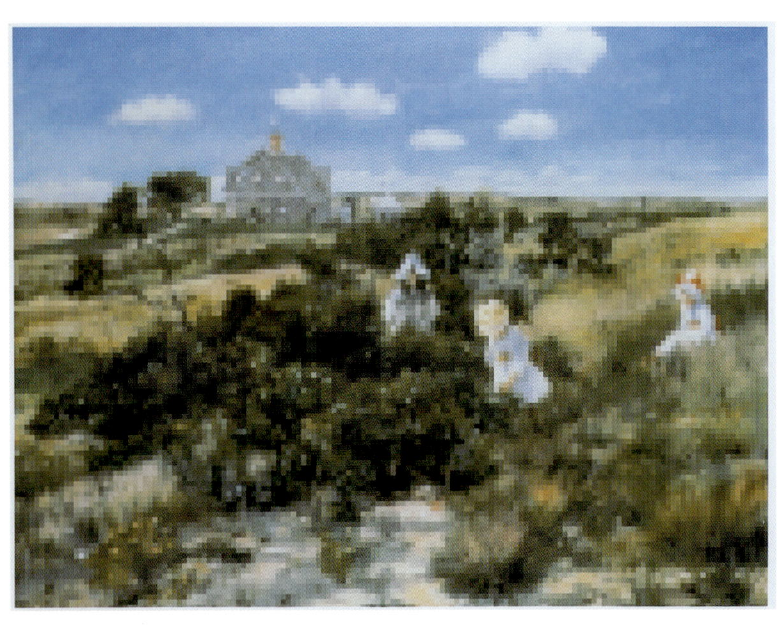

Above and facing page:
Artschwager's work in progress.

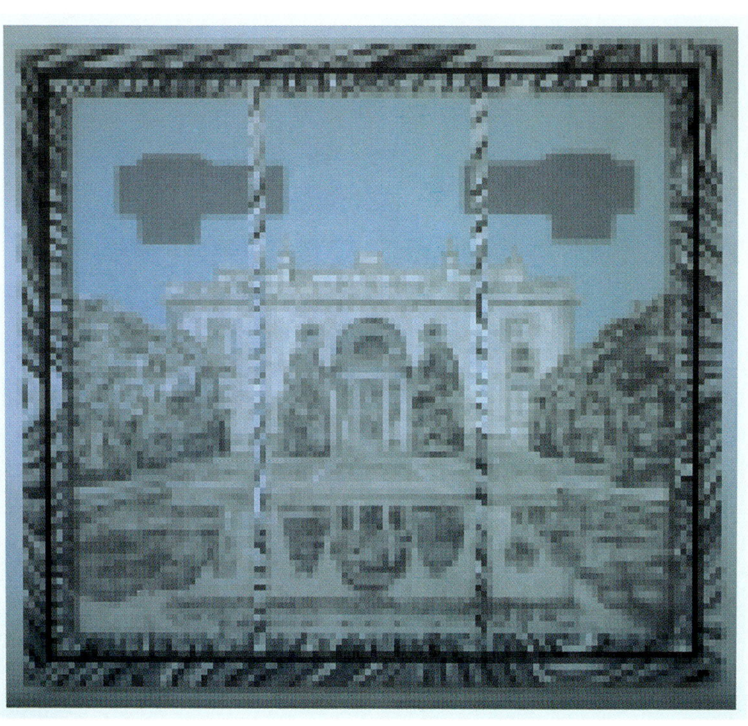

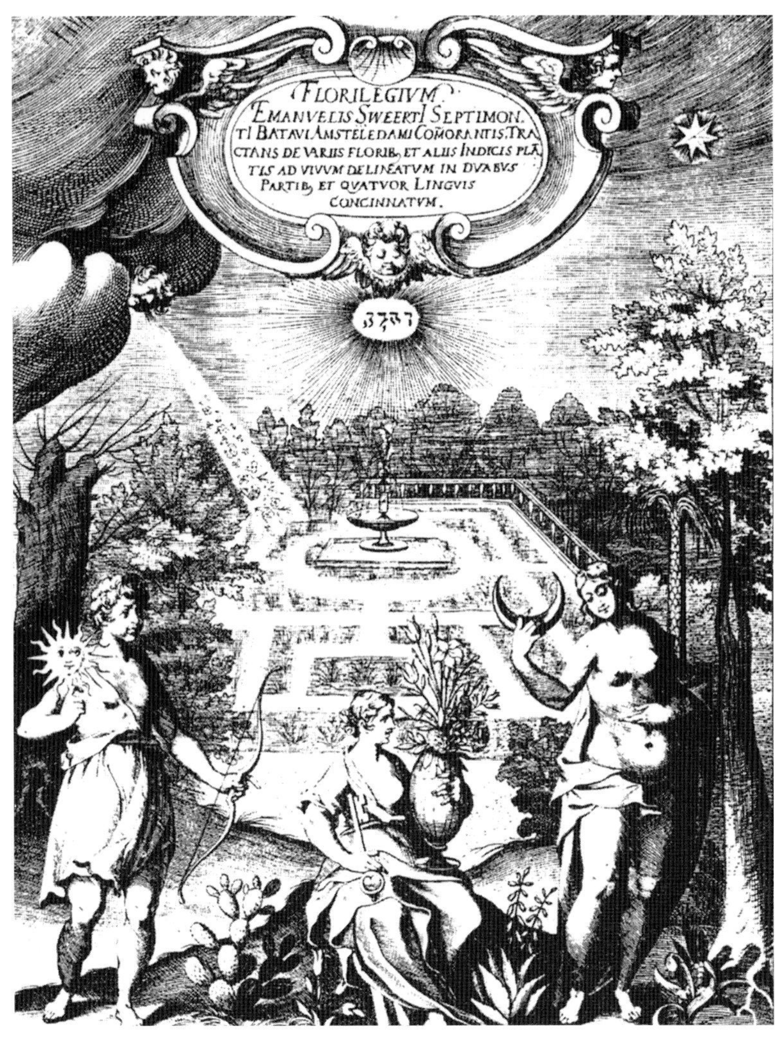

Seventeenth-century engraving submitted by Åsdam as source material for his work in progress.

KNUT ÅSDAM

Born in Trondheim, Norway, in 1968. Lives in Brooklyn, New York.

Knut Åsdam's media-based, environmentally scaled works probe and penetrate boundaries between private and public. To wit: At the 1999 Venice Biennale, he inserted into the Nordic Pavilion a cube of darkened outdoor space, complete with trees and meandering pathways, and replete with the magic and seediness of a ramble though a city park at midnight. From deep inside, one could see the rest of the exhibition and its viewers, while remaining invisible behind a reflective glass wall. A 1995 video, *Pissing*, perverted inside and out more intimately. A bloom of bodily fluid slowly leaked through and stained the front of the pelvic region of a man clad in tight-fitting pants. The pants were beige, a color that sets the tone for Åsdam's approach in general, which is neutral to cool. And yet one of the critical concepts informing his work, psychasthenia, comes from the literature of hysteria. The Surrealist Roger Caillois coined the term to describe a psychological state of "depersonalization by assimilation to space." For both Caillois and Åsdam, this sensation of letting one's identity lose itself in the environment is best described, and brought on, by the limitlessness of darkness.

Åsdam's first visit to the Parrish was less about seeing *The Bayberry Bush* than about sensing its context. We started at the beach, which on a windy autumn day was virtually empty—an open vista, especially compared with the landscape. The Hamptons is famous for its tall privet hedges that block the view from the road like a running green wall. "What is interesting," Åsdam later noted, "is of course that the houses here are often not visible." In light of which Chase's painting stands in "a very romantic relation to the surroundings and to nature, and to the American fictions of settlement." On the basis of the visit, Åsdam decided to comment on "the representation of property which is the dominant aspect of the work—so much so that the house has more detail than the faces of the children."

Åsdam's proposal takes the form of a dark chamber insulated for sound, with a video and aural element playing inside. In the process of developing these, he made another trip to Southampton, where he toured the Shinnecock Reservation, accompanied by the artist and resident David Bunn Martine. In lieu of privet hedges, this insular community barricades itself with a "Trespassers Will Be Arrested" sign that discourages access beyond the string of smoke shops along the public road front

(Native Americans can sell tax-free cigarettes on their own land). In his continued search for images of property, Åsdam plans to film the terrain from above, by balloon or airplane. His video may also include the seventeenth-century engraving he submitted with his proposal to illustrate "opulence, decadence, property, western culture and a romantic view of cultured nature," all of which he says have "quite a lot to do with the Hamptons." —I.S.

Readings

George Baker, "Piss Eloquent," *Artforum*, February 2000. Ina Blom, "Invitations to Stay," *NU, The Nordic Art Review*, no. 1 (1999). Ben Borthwick, "Over and Over Again, the Art of Knut Åsdam," in *End of Story, the Nordic Pavilion, the Venice Biennial 1999*, 1999. Ben Borthwick, "Queering Space," *Index*, March–April 1996. Brigitte Kölle, "Conversation with Knut Åsdam," in *Norden*, Vienna: Kunsthalle Wien, 2000. Mary Morlock et al., *Knut Åsdam Works 1995–2000*, London: Tate Britain, and Copenhagen: Galleri Tommy Lund, 2000.

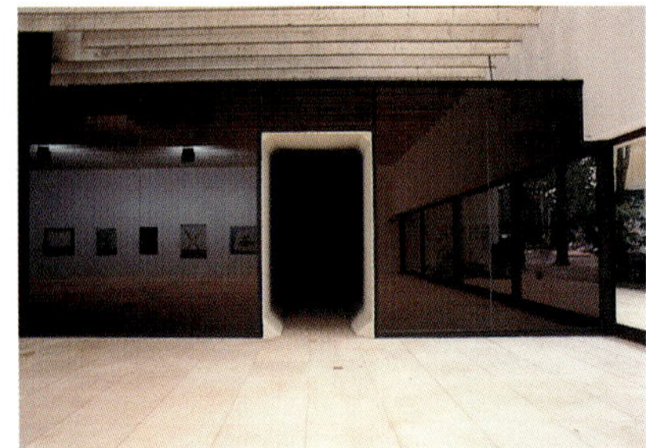

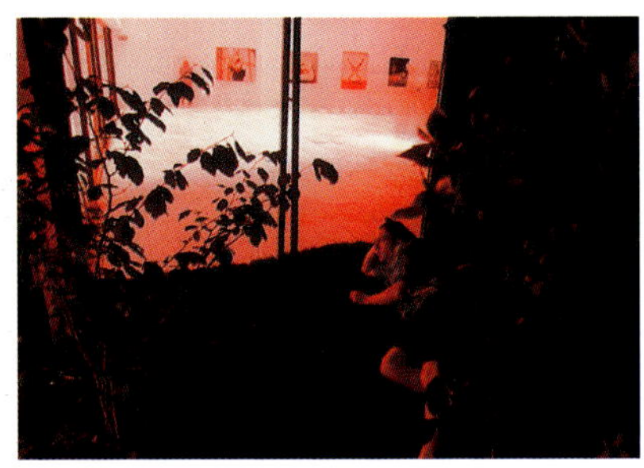

KNUT ÅSDAM, *Psychasthenia: The Care of the Self*, 1999. Filtered glass and garden, 10 x 25 x 40 feet. View of exterior, Nordic Pavilion, Venice Biennale.

Psychasthenia: The Care of the Self. Detail of interior.

CAI GUO-QIANG

Born in Quanzhou, China, in 1957. Lives in New York City.

In his room-size installation *Chase and Cai, Turtles and Time,* Cai Guo-Qiang meditates on time and history through the work of two fin-de-siècle artists (himself and Chase) presented in parallel. A selection of each artist's paintings, from Chase's Shinnecock period and Cai's student years, would hang salon style on flanking walls of a room at the Parrish. Chase's work would appear stable alongside Cai's experimental forms of figuration running the gamut of modernisms from Cubism to Expressionism. Yet that difference is perhaps less significant than the transformation within Cai's own art in the mid-eighties, when he began painting with gunpowder and then forsook canvas for earth and sky in site-specific performance pieces and interactive installations. A survey of these would be projected in rapid-fire slide and video images on a third wall. Made in far-flung cities from Taipei to Venice, Cai's politically attuned work shouts internationalism, while Chase remains the homebody, barely straying from the Shinnecock Hills. (This impression belies the fact that Chase, at least by nineteenth-century standards, was indeed a global artist, who regularly toured America and Europe.)

Amid this gallop of visual activity, eight live box turtles would quietly roam the gallery floor. And if the multimedia atmosphere became too much for them, they could seek refuge in one of the Chinese-style ceramic houses built by the artist and placed in the corners of the room.

This work is part of Cai's project of "rereading art history," which links politics to that history, often with a cross-cultural (specifically, Eastern versus Western) resonance. In *Still Life Performance,* at the 2000 Sydney Biennale, he invited several local artists to spend a week painting in the European section of the Art Gallery of New South Wales, where he had them set up their easels not in front of an old masterpiece but before a nude female model on horseback. With his clever shift of context, life drawing class became provocative performance art. Cai's use of theatrical, multivalent materials and images extends to explosives—known to him since childhood not only through his native province's famous manufacture of fireworks, but also, more ominously, from bombing during mainland China's conflict with Taiwan. In a spectacle staged in Vienna in 1999, a dragon inscribed in pink fire across the darkening sky represented both violence and beauty, tourism and terrorism, art and entertainment. The dragon, a symbol of power and prosperity to Asians, is seen by Westerners as a destructive force.

Turtles would seem relatively innocuous compared with explosives or nudes on horseback. But the reptiles can be carriers of salmonella, and in this antibacterial age, precautions must be taken. After extensive research into the possibility of having turtles range the gallery, the Parrish determined that the safety of both animal and human visitors would be compromised. To an alternative proposal of showing the turtles in an enclosed area, Cai responded that their "being confined . . . will inevitably give the impression of caged animals. This voyeuristic perspective is [the] opposite of the original idea where the turtles can roam freely in the gallery space and mingle with the visitor." —M.F.

Readings
Jane Farver and Reiko Tomii, *Cultural Melting Bath: Projects for the 20th Century*, New York: Queens Museum of Art, 1997. Yuko Hasegawa, *Cai Guo-Qiang: Chaos*, Tokyo: Setagaya Art Museum, 1994. Rosa Martinez and Yuko Hasegawa, *Cai Guo-Qiang I Am Y2K Bug*, Vienna: Kunsthalle Wien, 1999. Barry Schwabsky, "Tao and Physics: The Art of Cai Guo-Qiang," *Artforum*, Summer 1997. Dawei Sei, *Cai Guo-Qiang*, Paris: Fondation Cartier pour l'Art Contemporain, and London: Thames & Hudson, 2000.

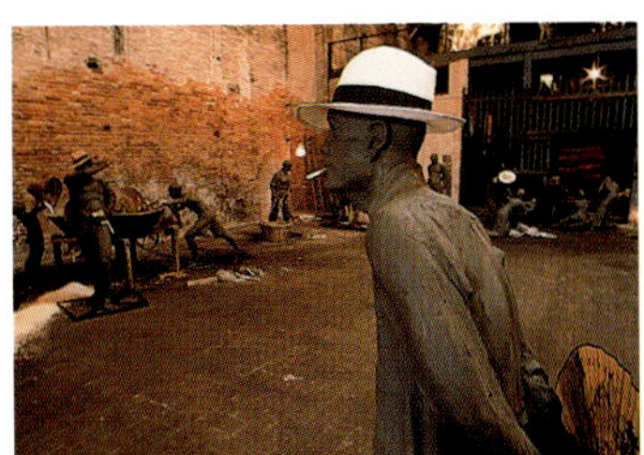

CAI GUO-QIANG, *Venice's Rent Collection Courtyard*, 1999, Venice Biennale.

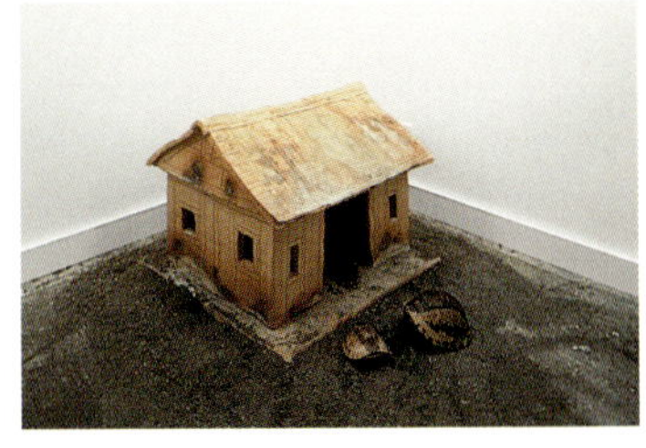

Promenade, 1994. Installation view, *Promenade in Asia* exhibition, Shiseido Gallery, Tokyo.

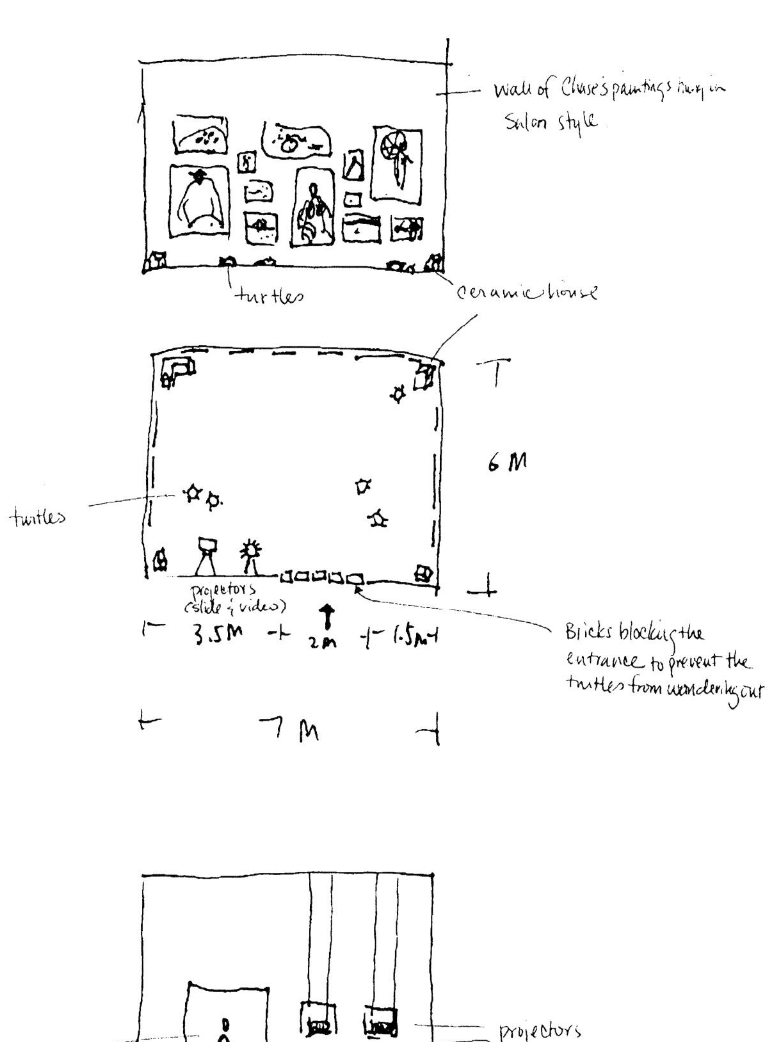

Drawing for the proposed *Chase and Cai, Turtles and Time.*

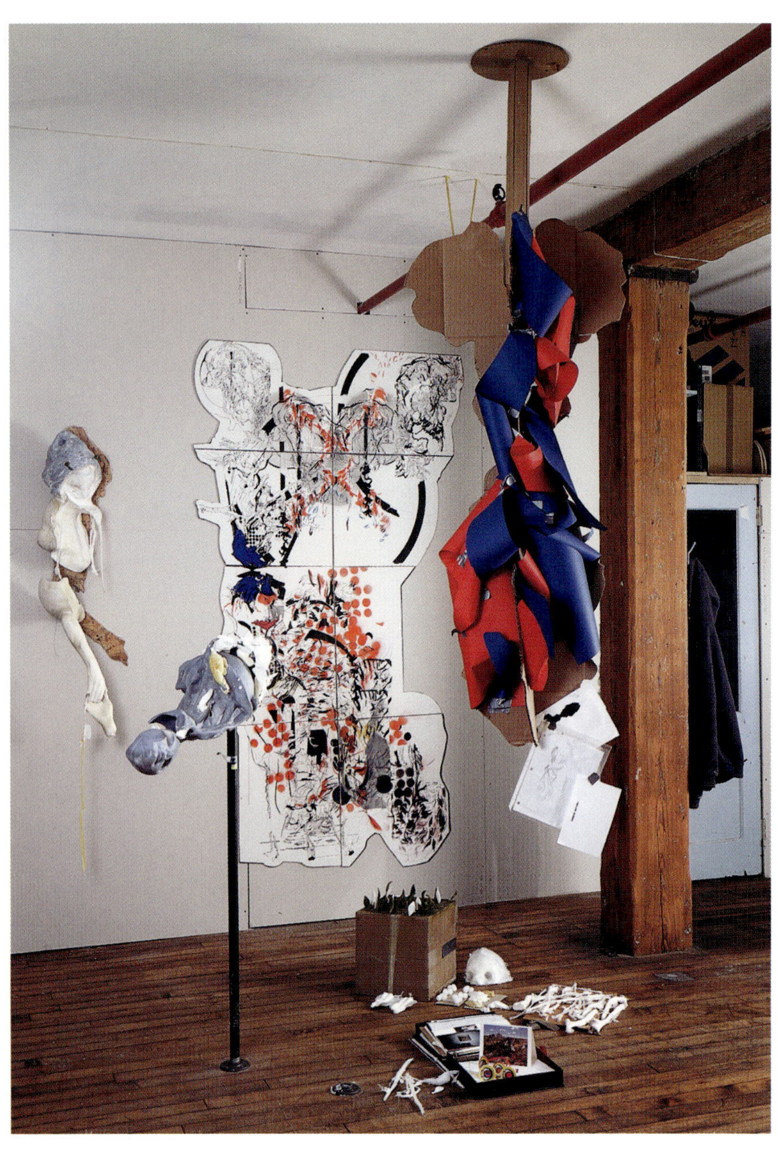

Studio view of Collura's work in progress.

BONNIE COLLURA

Born in Port Jefferson, New York, in 1970. Lives in Brooklyn, New York.

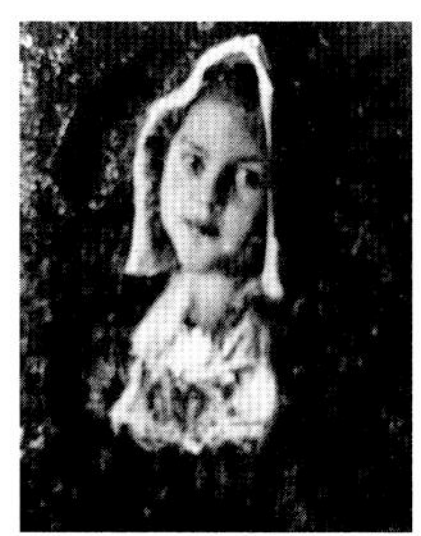

Photograph of a portrait of Helen Chase as Little Red Riding Hood, c. 1900. Gelatin printing-out paper, 2 7/8 x 2 inches. The William Merritt Chase Archives, The Parrish Art Museum, Gift of Mrs. A. Byrd McDowell.

Once Bonnie Collura overcame her resistance to the Impressionist style, she found abundant material in *The Bayberry Bush* to morph into shape. Collura builds her works from foam, plaster, putty, thick paint, and the surplus wealth of information in contemporary life—all funneled through her fascination with classical, folk, and indigenous mythologies, European art history, American popular culture, and the female protagonists throughout. The resulting sculptures are protean forms, caught between figuration and abstraction, at once futuristic and baroque. What pulled Collura (like so many other participating artists) into this project was material in the Chase Archives. In photographs of Chase's elaborately staged studio environments and *tableaux vivants*, Collura detected the sense of spectacle that has long attracted her to both Bernini and Walt Disney. Yet what really galvanized her was the notion that Chase's theatrics were preparations for the ultimate apotheosis—and the splashy Victorian funeral attending his death.

Out popped a three-part proposal, starting with a pair of 3-D glasses (Collura frequently works with triads) to be donned while viewing a sculpture (part two) suspended from the ceiling. The sculpture is based on the triangle plotted by the positions of the three girls in Chase's painting. On each of the points is an empty dress form, inspired by photographs from the Archives of girls dressed in the flowing robes of fantasy (as Red Riding Hood) and faith (in the devotional garb of Christian worship), and abstracted according to the reversing and doubling suggested by another Chase painting, *Alice in the Mirror*. Parts of the sculpture are painted in colors that Collura codes in her work as "abductor" red and "guardian" blue. These appear animated, alternately blocked and enhanced, by the 3-D glasses. The intended spectacle is of "ghostlike" forms—"inkblots"—tumbling through the gallery space. The third part of the installation is a tiara to be mounted on a wall somewhere in the museum. It will be a mix of head-gear found in Chase's work and the Archives, and local plant life. Collura titles this element of her installation *Helmet for Helen;* she calls the red and blue hanging sculpture *Anaglyph*.

What is the meaning of Collura's strenuous stretching, extrapolating, and reshaping? Although she sometimes provides keys or notes to clue viewers in to her iconography, she could not expect to convey all the ideas that directed her process here. On the one hand, her work is about subversion, about using information to level the authority and meaning of information, thereby reducing it to the abject or formless state her melting shapes embody. On the other, it's about transformation and exaltation, about taking something marginal, minor, or obscured and metamorphosing it into something of potentially heroic significance. Here the little girls are literally lifted from the past, where they appeared as flat, charming attributes of their father's landscape, a place rendered considerably less pat as envisioned by Collura. The girls are pumped up and skyed high, charged with the dynamics of provoking wonder and awe. —I.S.

Readings

Douglas Fogle, "Interview," in *Dialogues: Bonnie Collura/Santiago Cucullu,* Minneapolis: Walker Art Center, 2000. Janet Koplos, "Bonnie Collura at Basilico," *Art in America,* September 1998. Kim Levin, "Masters of the Universe," *The Village Voice,* May 23, 2000. Dominique Nahas, "Heads and Tails: Bodies of Thought/Bodies of Knowledge," *Review,* May 1, 1999. Suzanne Weaver, *Concentrations: Anne Chu and Bonnie Collura,* Dallas: Dallas Museum of Art, 1998.

BONNIE COLLURA, *Chain Reaction*, 1999. Fiberglass resin and paint.

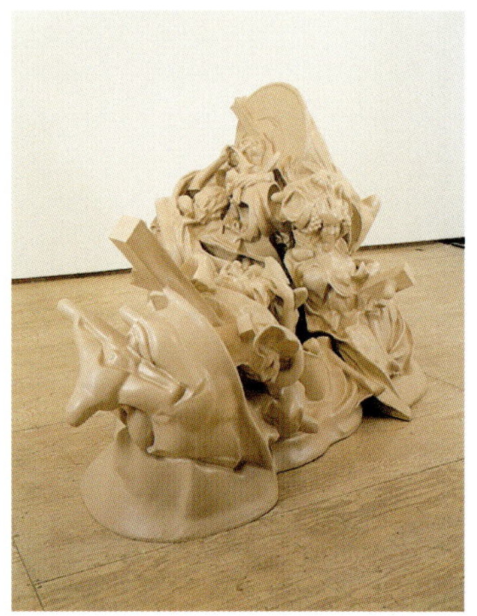

PETER DOIG

Born in Edinburgh, Scotland, in 1959; raised in Canada. Lives in London.

The only artist strictly dedicated to painting in the group, Peter Doig seemed a natural candidate for *About the Bayberry Bush.* His paintings frequently subsume the figure in the surrounding landscape. These quasi-folkloric views of forests and mountain lakes may derive from family holidays, whether more recent ones with his own children (three daughters, as it happens) or ski trips remembered from his youth in Canada. As in Chase's work, autobiographical material may inspire but is never the object of his painting.

Doig came to mind also because of his work's unusual relationship to postmodernism and tradition. Contemporary critiques charge painting with solipsism, sexism, and elitism, among other offenses; these charges would seem irrelevant to Doig, who favors process over politics. What does matter to him is how painting combines personal experiences and larger cultural influences. Doig's postmodernity lies in his recognition of the essential impurity of representation and in his allowing these filters—from his own memories and snapshots to travel ads, movies, and other art—to affect the pictorial product.

As in Impressionist views of the countryside, in which a distant steam engine pouring black smoke disrupts the sense of timelessness, roads, real estate, and tourism often figure in Doig's wildernesses. Ant-size skiers dot the side of a beautiful pink-toned, snow-covered mountain. The geometry of a Corbusian high-rise appears through a sinuous wood. Like so many hothouse flowers transplanted to that windswept terrain, Chase's daughters similarly represent modern life encroaching on the landscape.

Chase produced some of his most idiosyncratic works during the decade he summered in the Shinnecock Hills. He could have painted a nearby golf course or the idyllic shoreline (there are a handful of his renderings of the latter), subjects that are more conventionally picturesque. Instead, over and over he returned to scenes like that of *The Bayberry Bush,* with patchy underbrush, mangy bushes, strangely sloping foregrounds, and skewed horizon lines. These more rugged views dominate his Shinnecock period, and it is this New World, or perhaps North American, lack of refinement that Doig's work shares.

From the seashore to city parks, landscape in the late nineteenth century was considered the most modern of subjects, and painting *en plein air* the most sophisticated of methods. Of course, these are no longer stylish; Doig's paintbrush freezes when he takes it outside, so limiting does he find the unique perspective. (This is an artist who sets his process in motion by taking innumerable photographs of a given subject.) And the task of responding to a single painting proved constraining for him. As enthusiastic as he was about *The Bayberry Bush* and the project, he had to distance himself from both. After tucking away the notecard reproduction of Chase's painting, Doig pulled photographs of his daughters from his files. Yet in his search for a fabricated place, for what he calls the "idea of landscape," *The Bayberry Bush* was as good a place as any to start. —M.F.

Readings

Morris and Helen Belkin, *Peter Doig*, Vancouver: AA Gallery, University of British Columbia, 2001. Virginia Button, *The Turner Prize*, London: Tate Gallery, 1997. Leo Edelstein, "Peter Doig, Losing Oneself in the Looking," *Flash Art*, May–June 1998. Eva Meyer-Hermann et al., *Blizzard Seventy-seven*, Nürnberg: Kunsthalle Nürnberg, 1998. Adrian Searle, "The Twilight Zone," *The Independent*, October 21, 1994.

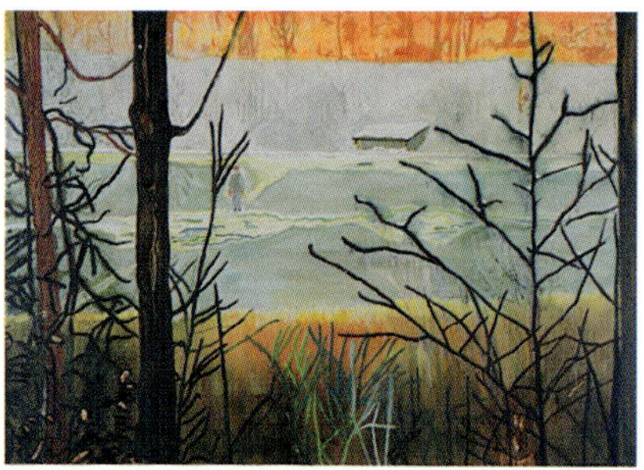

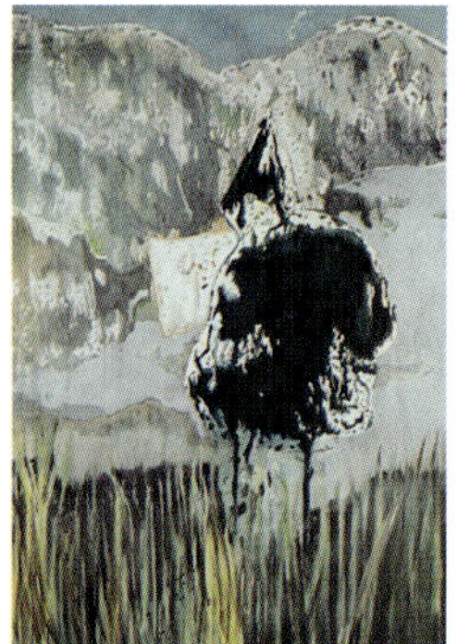

PETER DOIG, *Almost Grown*, 2000. Oil on canvas, 78 3/4 x 116 1/2 inches.

Figure in Mountain Landscape (I Love You Big Dummy), 1999. Oil on canvas, 106 x 77 inches.

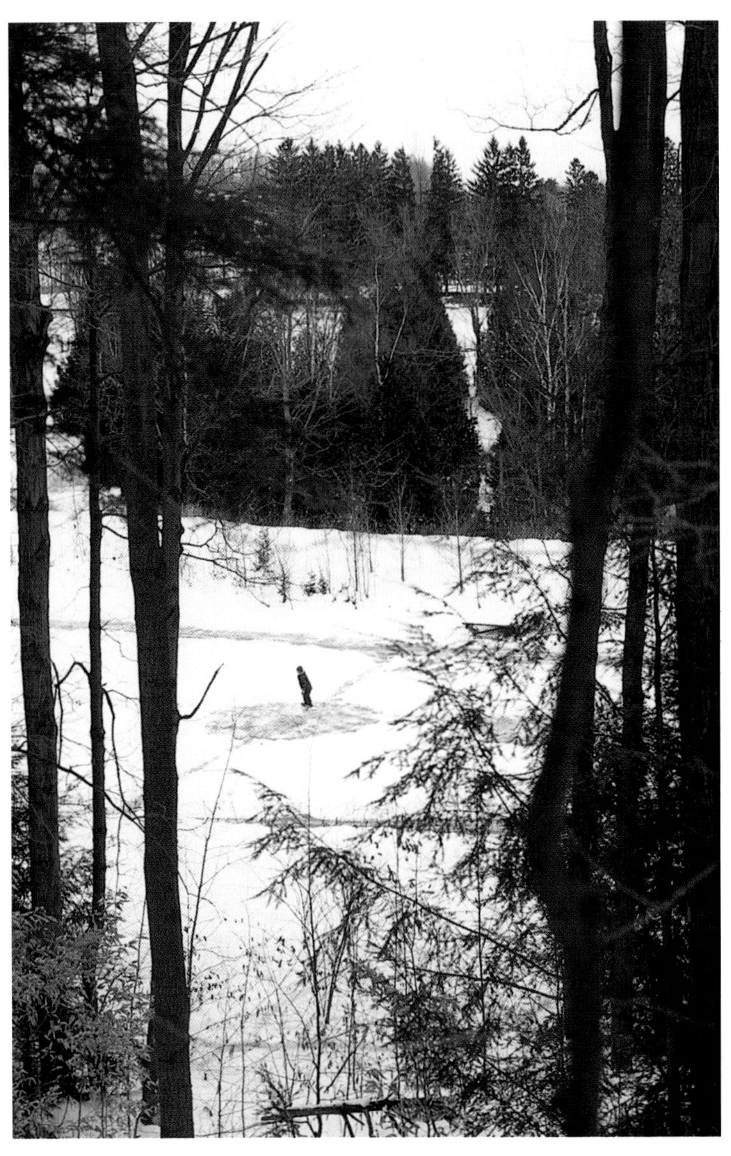

Photograph submitted by Doig for his painting in progress.

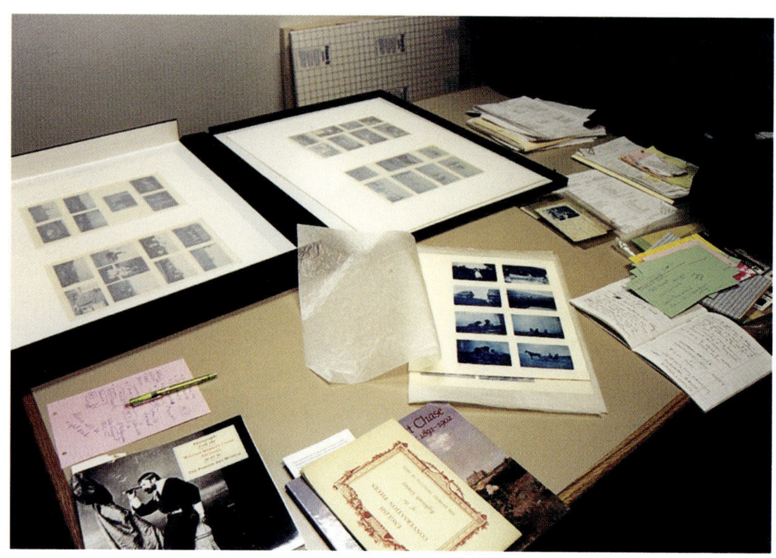

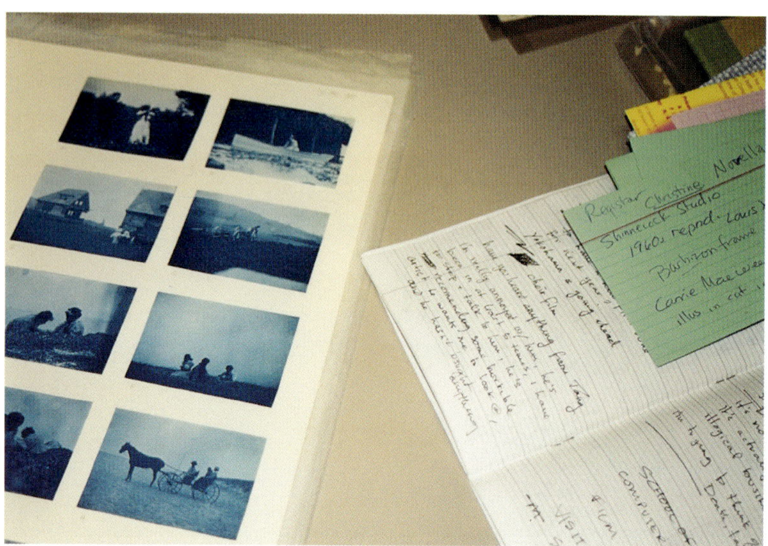

Photographs by Grigely of his work in progress, with material from the Chase Archives.

Facing page: The Chase children at play during summers at Shinnecock, 1908–1910. Cyanotypes, each c. 2 1/4 x 4 inches. The William Merritt Chase Archives, The Parrish Art Museum, Gift of Mrs. A. Byrd McDowell.

JOSEPH GRIGELY

Born in East Longmeadow, Massachusetts, in 1959. Lives in New Jersey.

Deaf since childhood, Joseph Grigely prefers reading notes to reading lips when conversing with non-signers. Knowing this, Ingrid and I came prepared with paper and pen to our first meeting with him. He talked. We wrote. As the conversation progressed, our notes became a patchwork of scrawled sentences crowding the paper, with writing turned this way and that, running around the corners and along the edges.

In the early 1990s, surveying the remains of a similar session of table-top graffiti, Grigely thought to start preserving these conversations (albeit only one side of them) on paper, and that was the beginning of his art. Selected notes may be mounted on the wall in an eye-catching constellation with the artist's typeset narrative alongside, or he may go so far as to reconstruct the setting by strewing the pen-and-paper trail across, say, a patio table, amid full ashtrays and empty beer bottles. He refers to these works as conversation pieces, after the pictorial genre, popular during the eighteenth century, in which sitters appear engaged in social activity.

In selecting specimens for his archives, Grigely covets the most offhand, banal remarks ("Another bottle?") that bring writing closest to talking. This spontaneous quality drew him to the photographs by Alice Gerson Chase that constitute the bulk of the Chase Archives. William Merritt Chase's wife, like Grigely, evidently sought to record the sociable side of life with her family of eight children. Her photographs capture them not only in mid-action (cavorting on the dunes, rolling in barrels) but also in mid-sentence. In one, the gaping space between a big sister and a little brother seems filled with her (ignored) request; in another, you can almost hear the beseeching tones of an older daughter, head cocked, arm outstretched, as she beckons the family dog slinking toward her. Grigely will choose a number of Alice Chase's cyanotypes

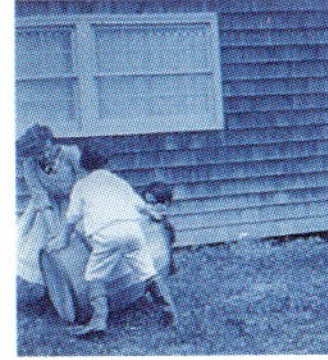

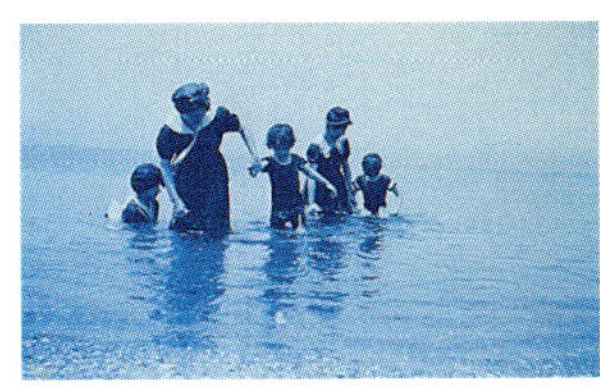

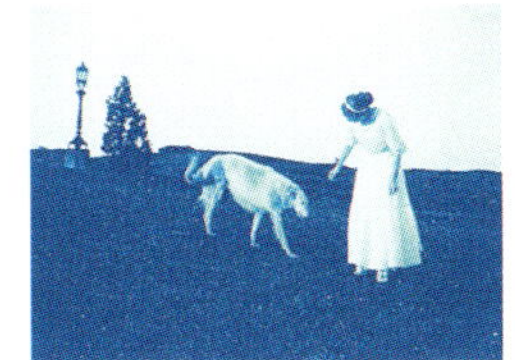

as the focal point of his project, which he plans as an illustrated publication made available to visitors in a reading room hung with some of her photographs juxtaposed with his conversation pieces.

Grigely's constant search for images of everyday speech brings to mind Chase's *Did You Speak to Me?* (see page 30), in which one of his daughters turns from a Shinnecock landscape she has been gazing at to look inquiringly toward the voice (and seemingly, the viewer) interrupting her reverie. *The Bayberry Bush,* for its part, emits not voices but the sound of wind and rustling petticoats. Aside from amplifying the conversational nature of this project as a whole, Grigely demonstrates, through the work of Alice Chase, the extent to which her husband's Shinnecock paintings relied on the daily life of his gregarious, growing family—its small talk and its silences. —M.F.

Readings

Nicolas Baume, "Text and Context: The Art of Joseph Grigely," in *Matrix 140: Joseph Grigely,* Hartford, CT: The Wadsworth Atheneum, 1999. Kate Bush, "Small Talk," *Frieze,* March–April 1996. *Conversation Pieces,* Kitakyushu, Japan: Center for Contemporary Art Kitakyushu, and Kyoto: Korinsha Press, 1998. Jan Estep, "Playing Footsie on Top of the Table: A Conversation with Joseph Grigely," *New Art Examiner,* June 2000. *Migrateurs,* Paris: Musée d'Art Moderne de la Ville de Paris/ARC, 1996.

JOSEPH GRIGELY, *9 Blue Conversations,* 2000. Ink and colored pencil on paper, and pins, 14 1/2 x 18 3/4 inches.

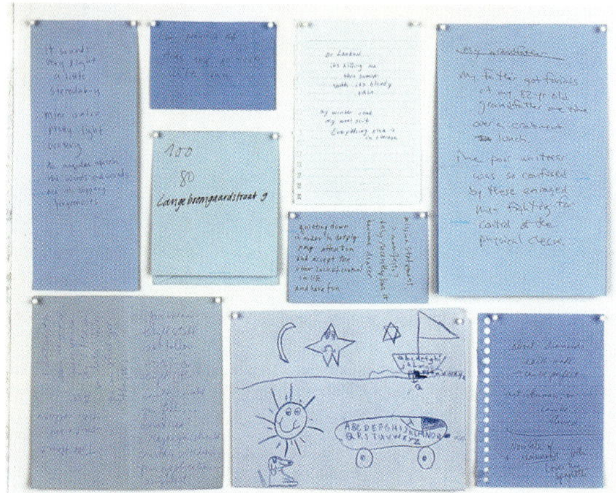

JITKA HANZLOVÁ

Born in Nachod, Czechoslovakia, in 1958. Lives in Essen, Germany.

Jitka Hanzlová's participation proves the armchair method of global curating. Melissa and I were introduced to her work in the catalogue of the 1996 Manifesta exhibition. Held in Rotterdam, this was the first in a series of surveys of contemporary art in Europe, slated to happen every two years, in ever-changing locations. (The next Manifesta will be held in Frankfurt.) We were taken by Hanzlová's photographs of people in landscapes that felt familiar, even folksy, yet alien. In one, a pair of boys (brothers?) in soiled T-shirts and jeans pose under a damp sky in a brown field, barely sprung green, with a large cottage in the distance. Despite its flatfooted contrast to Chase's painting of his daughters in the dunes—all leisure, sunshine, and white linen—it yielded surprisingly rich connections.

The photographs were shot in Rokytník, Hanzlová's childhood home, which she visited in 1995 and 1996, after ten years in exile. There she captured the general uneasiness of revisiting the past. But in her case it was increased by the gulf of differences between Western and Eastern Europe. These are apparent from a glimpse of the people (dressed in fashionless modern clothing as they set out to hunt, gather, till, play) and the landscape (cultivated fields and primitive forests), in photographs that cross the hardness with the vulnerability of culture outside industrial capitalism. In her most recent series, Hanzlová's sensitive gaze shifts from place to people: fifty-three images of women, from childhood to old age, throughout Europe and the United States. After the opening of an exhibition of these works in New York, Hanzlová visited the Parrish. She observed in Chase something of a kindred sensibility: "I come to the clear, short conclusion: Mr. Chase loved to make paintings about women, his children, environment, about his family and whatever was connected very closely to him, to his family." Driving around Southampton, she spotted a bayberry bush and stopped to photograph it.

Her proposal shows European landscapes. There's a wetness about them—they are misty, muddy—as well as a forlornness and a majesty. They bring out characteristics of Chase's landscape; this may or may not be intentional. Chase, a citizen of the New World, honed his vision while studying Old World culture and places. The Parrish owns a few of his Dutch scenes: one of polder farmland cut by canals, another of a peasant woman seated in a dark hut near a window. Thus far, none of Hanzlová's studies for the project includes figures. She is thinking about printing the works much larger than her usual small scale. In other words, she's still sketching. Who knows? She may yet be considering images of children at play, since a fanciful painted sketch by Chase of girls dressed as fairies, dancing in a line across a meadow, riveted her when she saw it in museum storage. —I.S.

Readings

Jeanne Greenberg, *Another Girl, Another Planet,* New York: Lawrence Rubin Greenberg Van Doren Fine Art, 1999. Jitka Hanzlová, *Female,* Hamburg: Deichtorhallen, and Munich: Mosel/ Schirmer, 2000. Jitka Hanzlová, *Rokytník,* Hardenberg, Germany: Museum Schloss Hardenberg, 1997. Robert Morgan, review of exhibition Jitka Hanzlová, *Female, New York Arts Magazine,* December 2000. Mathias Poledne, "I Want to Live Like Common People," in *Manifesta 1,* Rotterdam: Foundation European Art Manifestation, 1996.

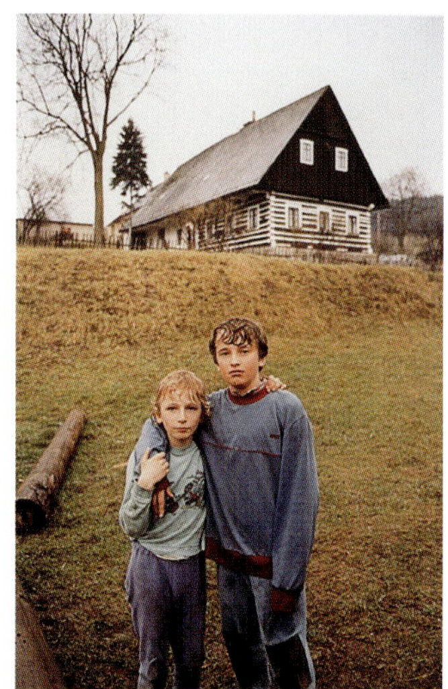

JITKA HANZLOVÁ, *Untitled (Cyril and Patrik), Rokytník,* 1993. Color print, 15 3/4 x 11 3/4 inches.

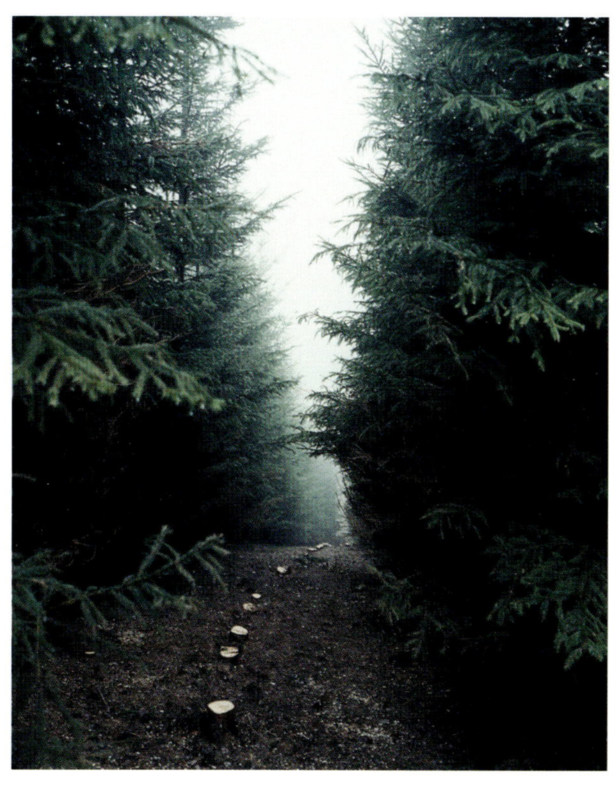

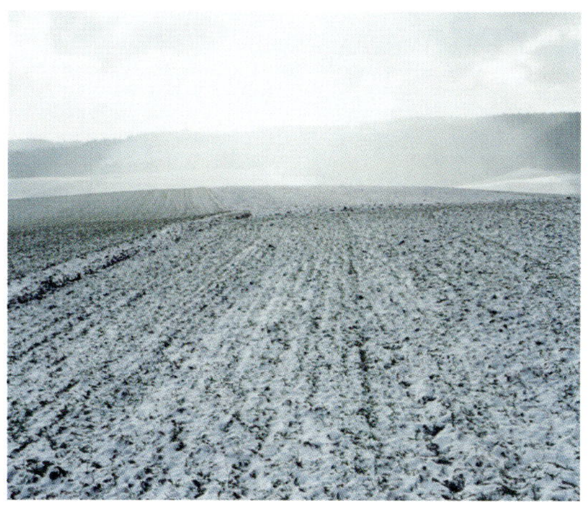

Photographs by Hanzlová for her work in progress.

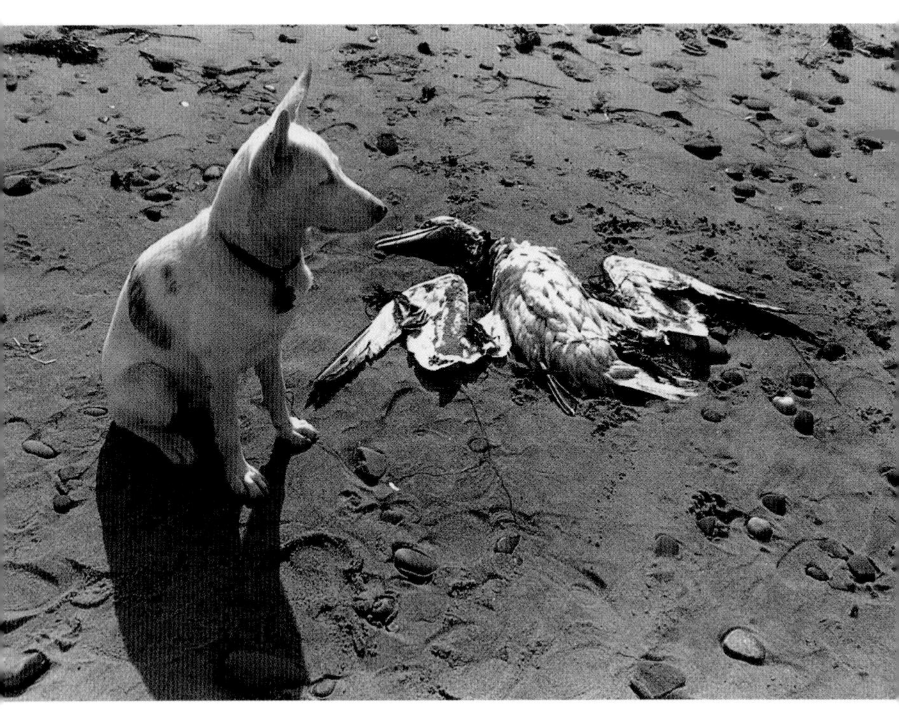

Photograph submitted by Jonas for her work in progress *Turn of the Century*.

JOAN JONAS

Born in New York City in 1936.
Lives in New York City.

Joan Jonas has made *tableau vivant* a viable, even radical, form of contemporary art since the 1960s, by using people (often herself) and props in living pictures, staged indoors and out, and produced as performance, film, and video. Her early involvement with these media makes her a pioneer, as does her feminism. She is her work's subject (traditionally, women were models not makers) and director (makers tended to be men). And although Jonas trained in art history, the pictures she builds are entirely new. They are also improvisational, and very much about the process of their own making.

Despite her qualifications for the exhibition, Jonas's project remains tentative. Thus far, I've received from her a photograph of her dog on the beach, and a title, *Turn of the Century*. These indicate her intent to keep things as open as possible, but they are full of significance to her art. Jonas has owned a number of white dogs, which figure in her work. Posed next to a dead pelican splayed on the sand, the dog in the photo seems almost to be sitting on a drawing of a bird in flight. Beaches means water, another standard in Jonas's art (and life: she spends summers on the coast of Nova Scotia). Early titles include *Jones Beach* and *Oad Lau* (or "watering place," named after a Moroccan village). *Volcano Saga* was shot in Iceland, where Jonas was struck by how naturally people spent their time talking in hot springs; she directed her actors to do the same. In this film, she wanted to show landscape as psychic space, a desire that is implied in her many images of figures approaching from a great distance, and that reminds me, in this instance, of the void that is the dunescape of *The Bayberry Bush*.

Jonas has remarked on her attraction to water's reflective surface and to mirrors. The mirror, of course, brings us back to one of the earliest metaphors for painting. And it leads also to video's early history, when Jonas and others were suddenly freed from the constraints of filmmaking and could tape themselves performing in their studios. Jonas's most famous mirror work is a film, *Mirror Check* (1970), based on a performance in which she manipulates a hand mirror to inspect every inch of her nude body. Relations between women and mirrors have long been the stuff of legend, and to construct her work, Jonas quotes from narratives of all kinds: sagas, songs, fairy tales, opera, poetry, the news, and cultural and historical accounts.

Travel, music, and exotic costuming are likewise important aspects of her process.

How she will elaborate on *The Bayberry Bush,* one can only guess. This is typical of Jonas's work, which is founded on faith and daring, trust and risk. That goes for all involved in it. Ultimately, working without boundaries (or a safety net) is what keeps things interesting for her, and for us. —I.S.

Readings

Douglas Crimp, ed., *Joan Jonas: Scripts and Descriptions 1968–1982,* Berkeley, CA: University Art Museum, 1983. Andre Jahn, *Joan Jonas Performance Video Installation 1968–2000,* Stuttgart: Galerie der Stadt Stuttgart and Cantz, 2000. Joan Jonas with Rosalind Krause, *Seven Years, The Drama Review,* March 1975. Dorine Mignot, *Joan Jonas: Works 1968–1994,* Amsterdam: Stedelijk Museum, 1994. Joan Simon, "Variations: An Interview with Joan Jonas," *Art in America,* July 1995.

JOAN JONAS, *Organic Honey (Visual Telepathy),* 1972. Gelatin silver print, 11 x 14 inches.

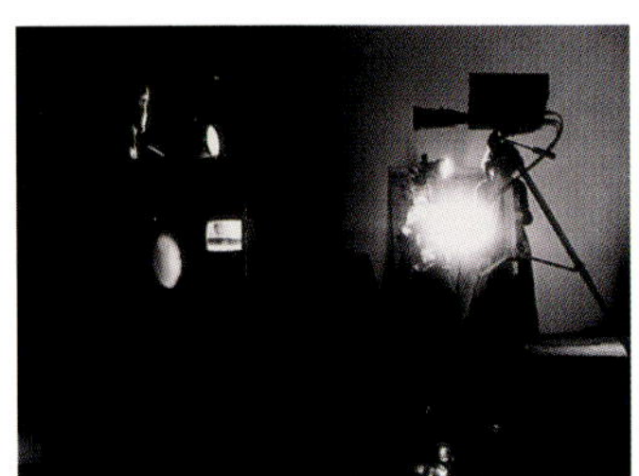

Scene from *Volcano Saga,* 1987, Performing Garage, New York.

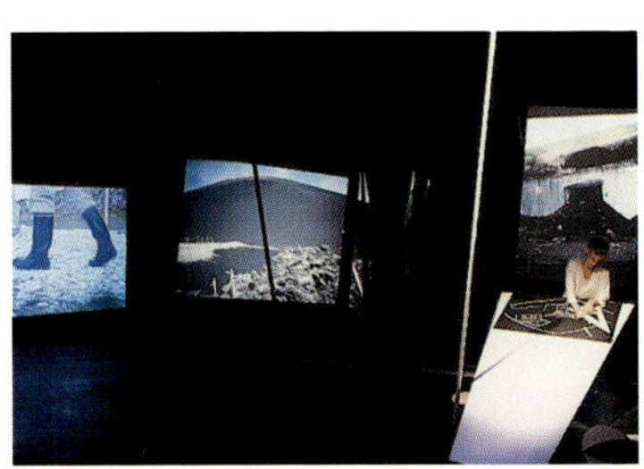

LEE MINGWEI

Born in Taichung, Taiwan, in 1964. Lives in New York City.

What are the Chase daughters thinking, Lee Mingwei wonders. And what will become of these three little girls? In *The Bayberry Bush* they function as a charming formal device, puppets to their father's conception of landscape and leisure. But to Mingwei, this pictorial instance of children's subjection to a parent's vision stands as a paradigm of the outside pressures that can thwart a young person's search for selfhood. Most adults, the artist says in his proposal, "come to do what society (especially friends and relatives) expects of them, rather than what they feel (or once felt) would really make them happy."

When I Grow Up gives voice, symbolically, to the Chase girls and to the muted or lost child in all of us. Mingwei's video installation consists of a series of filmed interviews with "children" of all ages (roughly four to eighty years old). To each he poses the question: "What would you like to be when you grow up?" The color videotape will be presented cinema style, projected large on the wall of a darkened room. The responses constitute a moment of self-representation in which the subjects picture themselves as—or indeed are—children, unformed by adult expectations. Mingwei tries to catch people off guard, for a spontaneous, gut response. Camcorder in hand, he approaches prospective subjects (most of whom won't know him) in a park, at a gallery, or on the street for on-the-spot interviews.

Making people feel comfortable seems to be one of the artist's great gifts. For a recent project, he enlisted people he didn't know to spend the night with him alone (in separate beds) in a New York gallery he had set up like a Japanese dorm room. Participants in the *The Letter-Writing Project* (1998) underscored the cathartic aspect of his work by penning the letter to someone living or dead that they had been "putting off with excuses," in one of the private booths set up in the exhibition area. Some writers chose to display their letters unsealed, for others to read, on ledges lining the walls of the serene, Asian-style minimalist spaces. Whether people are spending a night with the artist or offering a confidential letter as part of a public collection and ceremony, Mingwei's works are brought to fruition by volunteers whose reactions and recollections form a contemplative public archive of his design.

The concept for *When I Grow Up* derives from Ch'an Buddhism, which Mingwei studied as a child, and whose humble rituals, simplicity of means, and introspective nature have lent a distinctive character to his brand of conceptualism. His question relates to the koan, a form of inquiry the Ch'an student must negotiate as an exercise toward achieving enlightenment. There is no "right" or direct explanation for the koan, but rather one that testifies to a profound level of insight. Likewise, the question posed in this piece is a tool for gaining access to a fundamental wish or state of being. Mingwei's "What would you like to be when you grow up?" invites every viewer of Chase's 106-year-old painting to dream of the future. —M.F.

Readings

Jennifer Gross and Lewis Hyde, *Lee Mingwei: The Living Room,* Boston: Isabella Stewart Gardner Museum, 2000. Kay Larson, "To Take Part in the Art, You Sleep with the Artist," *The New York Times,* November 5, 2000. Roxana Marcoci, "The Social Factor of Public Art: Lee Mingwei in Conversation with Roxana Marcoci," in *Lee Mingwei: 1994–1999,* Cleveland: Cleveland Center for Contemporary Art, 1999. Lee Mingwei, "The Dining Project: The Art of Nurturing," *Tricycle: The Buddhist Review,* Fall 1997. Eugenie Tsai, *Way Stations: Lee Mingwei,* New York: Whitney Museum of American Art, 1998.

LEE MINGWEI, *The Dining Project (Lombard-Freid),* 1997. Wood, audiotape players, tableware, beans, rice, and tatami mats, 132 x 132 x 24 inches.

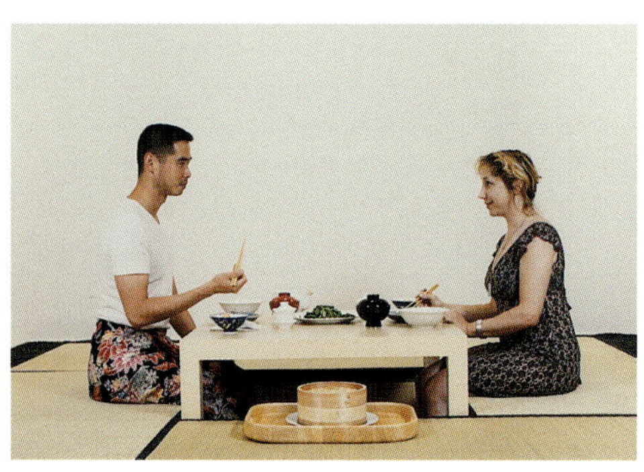

Facing page: Graduation photograph of Mingwei's grandmother Lin Wanyue, one of the first Taiwanese women doctors in Western medicine, 1920, submitted by the artist for his work in progress.

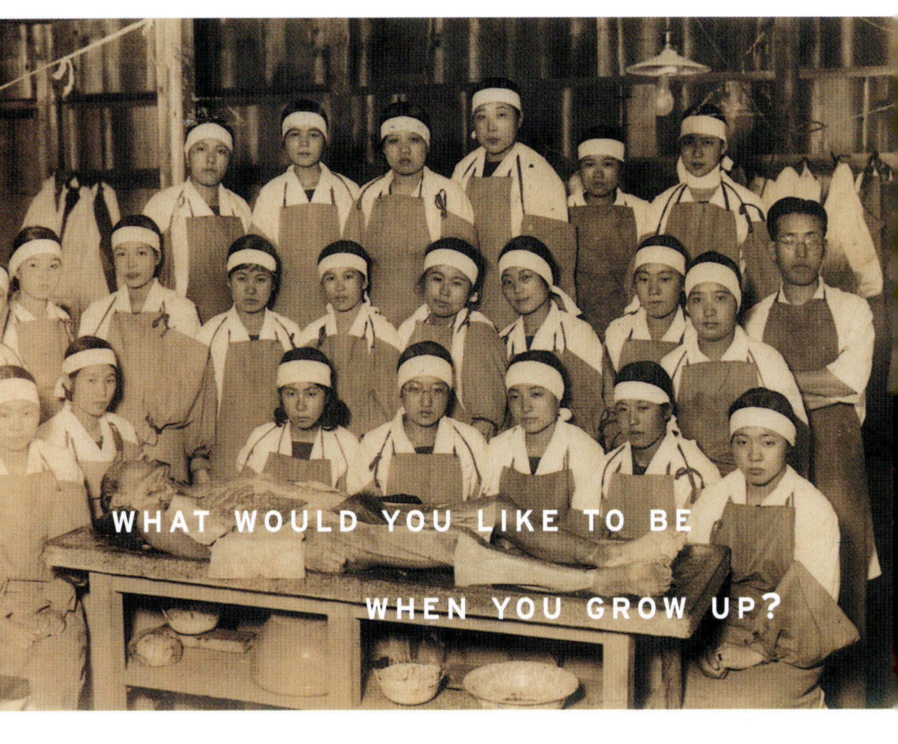
WHAT WOULD YOU LIKE TO BE
WHEN YOU GROW UP?

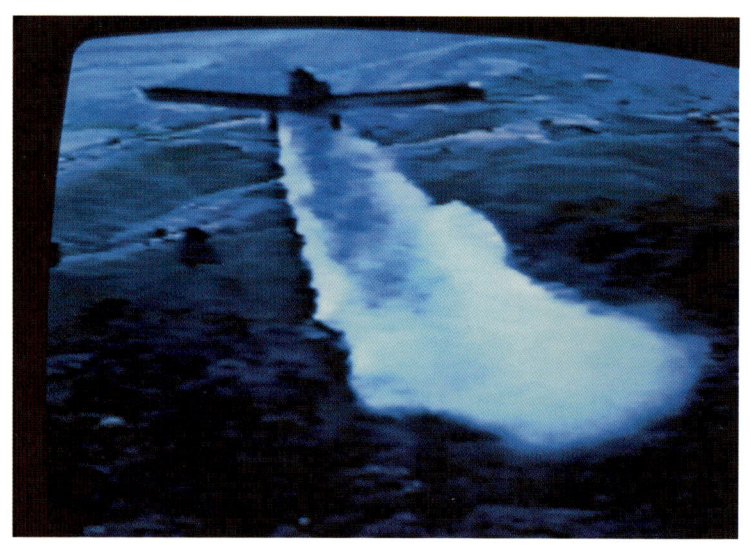

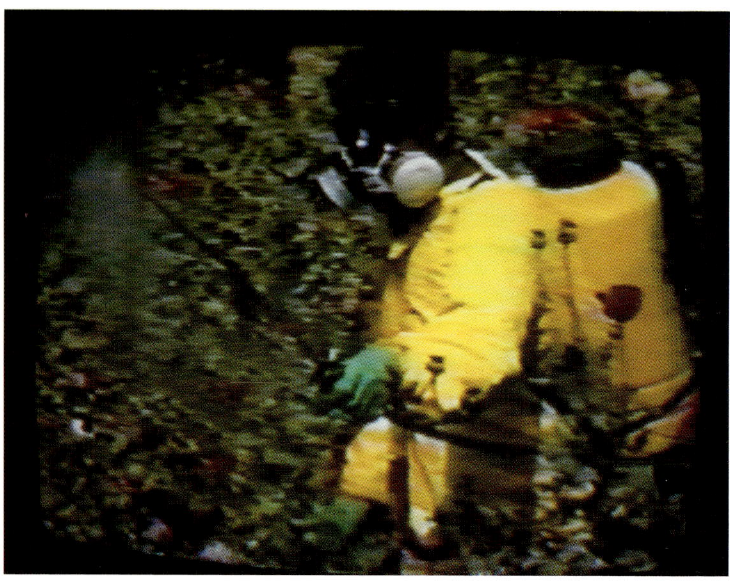

Video stills from Restrepo's work in progress *Psychotropic Impressionism*.

JOSÉ ALEJANDRO RESTREPO

Born in Paris in 1959.
Lives in Bogotá, Colombia.

Jump cut from the nineteenth-century North American landscape represented by William Merritt Chase to a twenty-first-century South American one composed by José Alejandro Restrepo. Billowing clouds of white chemicals stream from airplanes that streak across blue sky. A figure in a field of poppies hand-fumigates the crop. These images are projected as three videos—two pointed skyward and the other toward the floor—with a sound track billed in the artist's proposal as "Impressionist Music." The ambience reconciles Restrepo's detached depiction of traffic and labor to Chase's dreamy painting by way of a dialectic of drugs.

Restrepo's installations are typically sites of engagement between natural and native history, consumer and colonial cultures. In a work from 1993–1996, bunches of live bananas, practically the size of adults, hung from the ceiling of a dramatically lit space, while on the walls, images and texts presented early European perceptions of South American peoples—as lazy and apathetic—read through plantain, a nourishing dietary staple plentiful across the tropics. The plantain's scientific name, *Musa paradisiaca* (also the title of the piece), evokes Judeo-Christian mythology. In the garden of Eden, the tree symbolized good and evil: What fruit, the artist pondered, did Eve really bite from? In the realm of present-day life, Restrepo's piece touched on the metaphor of the banana republic: an economy based on the exploitation of human and natural resources—no paradise on earth.

From the inception of his project for this exhibition, Restrepo knew he wanted his work to assert his identity as a Colombian artist by establishing clear contrasts: "North–South, bucolic and bourgeois landscape vs. a wild and contradictory (human and natural) landscape." He also immediately determined the structure of the installation. His idea for the imagery, however, underwent some change. Restrepo's preliminary proposal was based on the legend of Avelino, the last porter in the Colombian jungles of Chocó, and pitched the question: Who carries whose weight in a master–slave relationship? Conceptually and visually, the work promised to stand strong on its own. But in terms of the big picture, *About the Bayberry Bush,* would the contrasts outweigh the comparison to be drawn between Colombian and American landscapes about colonialism? My curatorial concerns may or may not have been justified, or shared by the artist, who, in any case, shifted his focus. (Nor may he have known this curiosity: In South America, some of the chemicals sprayed to kill drug crops are killing off bayberry bushes as well, and thus adversely affecting today's candle-making industry.)

Restrepo's title for his installation at the Parrish, *Psychotropic Impressionism,* is the finishing twist. The adjective *psychotropic,* which refers to an action on the mind, is often used to describe drugs. Thus the tranquillity for which *The Bayberry Bush* is famous induces the pleasantly and dangerously numbed perceptions represented by Restrepo's imagery of narcotics production. In reality, an imagery as volatile as any landscape of war. —I.S.

Readings

Carlos Basualdo, "Cocodrilos o los Project Rooms Latinoamericanos," *ARCO Noticias* (Madrid), no. 1, May 1988. Natalia Gutiérrez, "Arte Colombiano. Cruces," *Atlántica, Internacional Revista de las Artes* (Canary Islands), no. 15 (Winter 1996). José Alejandro Restrepo, *Colombia,* São Paulo: XXIII Bienal Internacional de São Paulo, 1996. José Alejandro Restrepo, *Musa Paradisiaca: Una Video-Instalación,* Bogotá: Museo de Arte Moderno de Bogotá, 1997. José Roca, *Context,* New York: Apex Art Curatorial Program, 2000.

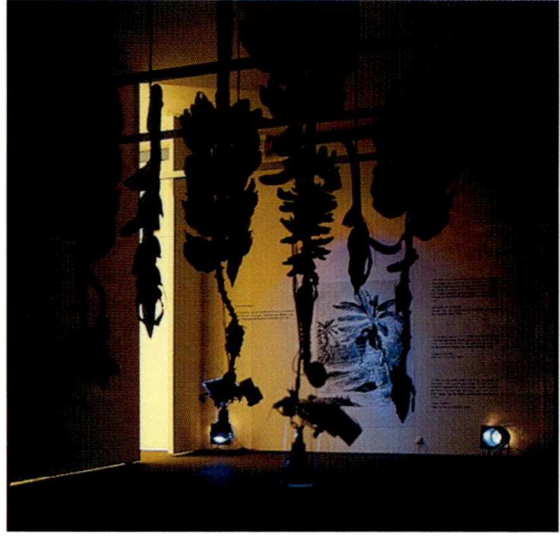

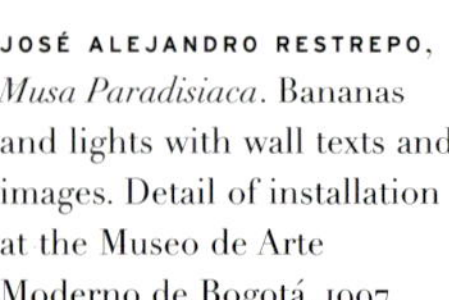

JOSÉ ALEJANDRO RESTREPO, *Musa Paradisiaca.* Bananas and lights with wall texts and images. Detail of installation at the Museo de Arte Moderno de Bogotá, 1997.

BEVERLY SEMMES

Born in Washington, D.C.
Lives in New York City.

For Beverly Semmes, it all boils down to land and sky. Put green below and blue above and you have landscape. But instead of Chase's oil paint on canvas, what if the land consists of very big ceramic pots, a grove of them at your feet, and the sky—a blue so saturated it has the bottomless quality of lapis lazuli—appears as the shimmering dress worn by a barefooted wanderer?

So goes the footage in Semmes's *Around the Shinnecock Pots,* in which the artist, camera in hand, has videotaped herself stepping through this odd terrain. As outlandish as it may appear, the mise-en-scène does approach the remoteness of the painting's windswept dunes. Are chunky pots and silky gowns any more improbable than Chase's dainty daughters around that beastly bush? The videotape is shown on a four-by-five-inch screen, about the size of a children's book illustration or a daguerreotype, a miniature all the better in its intimacy for expanding the imagination. The pots themselves, around eight in all, reappear as an independent sculptural installation elsewhere in the gallery. They will be painted grass-green or, more abstractly and unnaturally, a fluorescent orange.

A simple, slightly comic grandeur characterizes Semmes's thinking about the body/vessel, nature, and space—matters that have interested her for the past decade. In previous works, wall-mounted dress forms in such fanciful fabrics as organza and crushed velvet warp into towering columns or waterfalls whose overflowing folds might fill the gallery floor. This reassessment of the figure-ground relationship, in which the figure (usually female) merges with architectural space or the vastness of nature, has been an expression of empowerment—Semmes's roots are feminist—and the reassessment continues in the video.

Around the Shinnecock Pots assumes the girls' vantage point, and puts them in control of the image and the viewer in the thick of that underbrush. In staging a *tableau vivant* the three girls themselves might enact, the artist commands every role: set designer (the hand-built pots), costume designer (the dress), model/actress, director, and camera operator. Rather than paint it, Semmes interprets the image in terms of things she likes to do, activities that also represent the traditional domain of women's creativity: sewing and ceramics. The video also hints at latent elements of Chase's work and working process. Think of the painter's stagy studios and his penchant for dress-up (private theatrics recorded in photographs taken by his wife), as well as his ready absorption of the dramatic cropped shot introduced by photography. Plein-air painting was as close as an Impressionist could get to the immediacy of such later time-based forms as video and performance art.

Initially Semmes wanted to make a "real" *tableau vivant* by having a live model in the blue gown interact with the pots in the gallery. Instead, the pots are to be shown alone; the videotape will also occupy a space of its own. Semmes decided the presence of a live model might distract from the viewer's mental walk around the Shinnecock pots. —M.F.

Readings

Connie Butler, "Terrible Beauty & the Enormity of Space," *Art + Text,* 1993. Amada Cruz, *Options 50: Beverly Semmes,* Chicago: Museum of Contemporary Art, 1995. Melissa Feldman, *Beverly Semmes,* Philadelphia: Institute of Contemporary Art, University of Pennsylvania, 1993. Bruce Ferguson, "Beverly Semmes: Location, Location, Location," in *Beverly Semmes: New and Recent Sculpture,* Dublin: Irish Museum of Modern Art, 1997. Patricia Phillips, *Beverly Semmes,* London: Camden Art Centre, 1994. Ingrid Schaffner, "Heavenly Body," in *Beverly Semmes "Not Here,"* Middletown, CT: Ezra & Cecile Zilka Gallery, Wesleyan University, 1999.

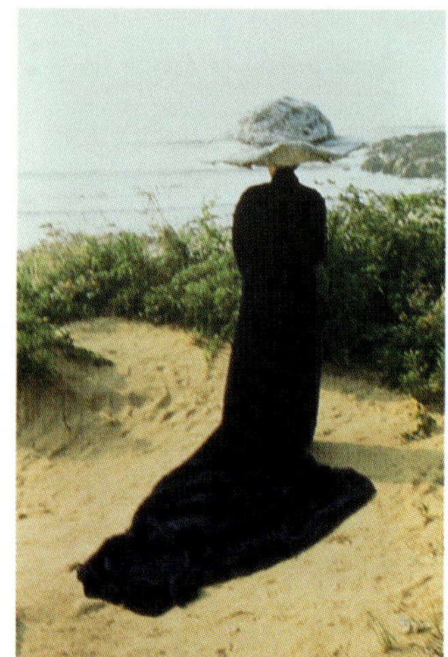

BEVERLY SEMMES, *Figure in Purple Velvet Bathrobe and Cloud Hat,* 1991. Color print, 10 x 8 inches.

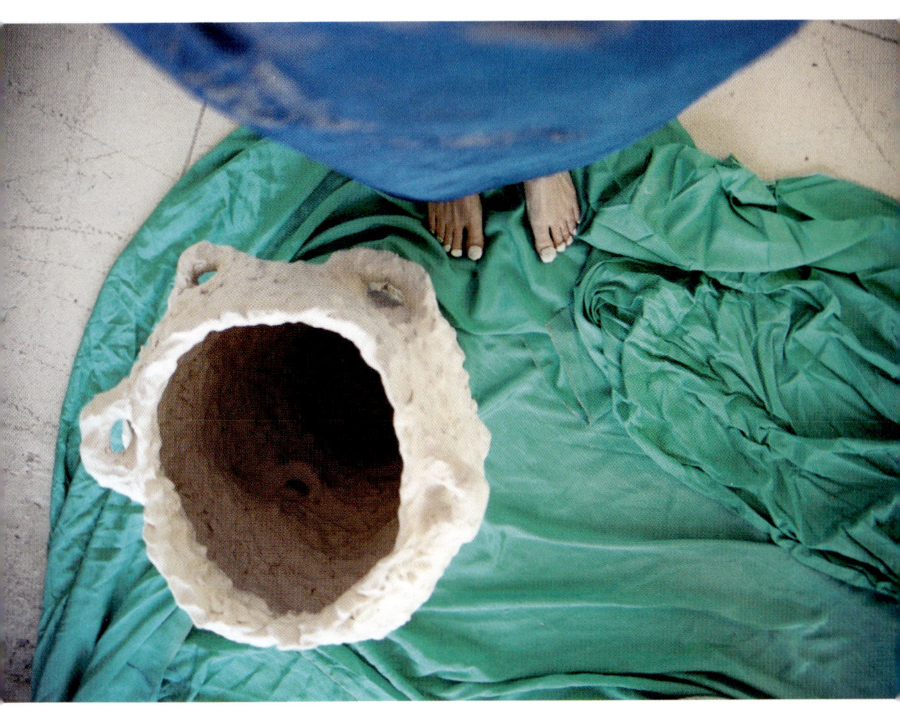

Photograph by Semmes of her work in progress *Shinnecock Pots*.

YUTAKA SONE

Born in Shizuoka, Japan, in 1965.
Lives in South Pasadena, California.

The Bayberry Bush is a passport to Yutaka Sone's own happiest mental and pictorial destination: the jungle. Chase's fetching view of children, vegetation, and sunlight—all of which Sone counts among his favorite things—affected this Japanese conceptual artist enough that he bypassed analytical routes into the painting. What he offers in his installation is a parallel universe to Chase's, a place of refuge, beauty, and freedom.

In the installation, a half-dozen of Sone's "jungle paintings" hang on the walls of a room. One might need a machete to see them, however, obscured as they are by a thicket of tropical-looking potted plants. The leafy, sun-drenched images can be spied from a trail cleared through the dense foliage. With their broad, lush brushstrokes that turn the plants into fat green spiders, Sone's jungle paintings resemble children's Craypas drawings. The naive effect is not at all contrived, but has a Fauvist exuberance and intensity about it.

Sone sees no difference between a painted landscape and an actual one, or for that matter, between a realized work and an unrealized one (many of his creations exist only as proposals on paper or as models). "They give me the same feelings," he explains. His thinking beyond traditional definitions or limits relates, appropriately, to the jungle: "There are no places to sit down, no floors, no walls, no physical boundaries, no left, no right. . . . I get a feeling of something unfinished and unknown."[1]

To evoke this expansiveness, Sone's mixed-media installations and public projects always involve travel and motion—means to disrupt the stasis of the art object and make viewing art a time-based, physical experience. His *Bayberry Bush* installation must be felt and heard by the viewer, who pushes and swishes through live foliage to reach the painted landscapes hidden beyond. Sone has plans for large-scale works in which people would zoom past his paintings, riding on roller coasters or sliding down ski slopes—moving pictures in which the viewer moves, not the images. He seems to liken the frisson of the encounter with beauty to the thrill of a Great Adventure ride.

One might think of this fleeting glimpse of the art as a carnivalesque notion of Impressionism, through which painting found a new effervescence. Certainly the children and the greenery in *The Bayberry Bush* are symbols of growth and change. Yet the civilian elements—the gray geometry of the house, the girls' confectionary clothing—are harbingers of other changes: namely, the stylish holidaymaking and rampant real estate development soon to overtake the Shinnecock Hills. In our own era of tourism, when nature itself needs to be preserved like a museum object, perhaps Sone is right—there is no difference between real nature and artificial nature, as long as they both give you that "feeling." —M.F.

1. From an interview with the artist by Hans-Ulrich Obrist in *La Ville/Le Jardin/La Memoire* (Rome: Académie de France à Rome, 2000), p. 28.

Readings

Yuko Hasegawa, *The Man Who Digs a Bottomless Swamp—or, An Absurd Duchamp,* Tokyo: Yokohama Galleria, 1994. Min Nishihara, *Building Romance,* Tokyo: Mitaka City Arts Foundation, 1996. Min Nishihara, "Tokyo by Night," *Siksi,* Summer 1998. Lars Nittve and Shin Kurosawa, *Nutopi,* Malmö, Sweden: Rooseum, 1995. Hans-Ulrich Obrist, *La Ville/Le Jardin/La Memoire,* Rome: Académie de France à Rome, 2000.

YUTAKA SONE, *Amusement*, 1998. Carved marble and plants, 18 1/2 x 25 5/8 x 15 inches.

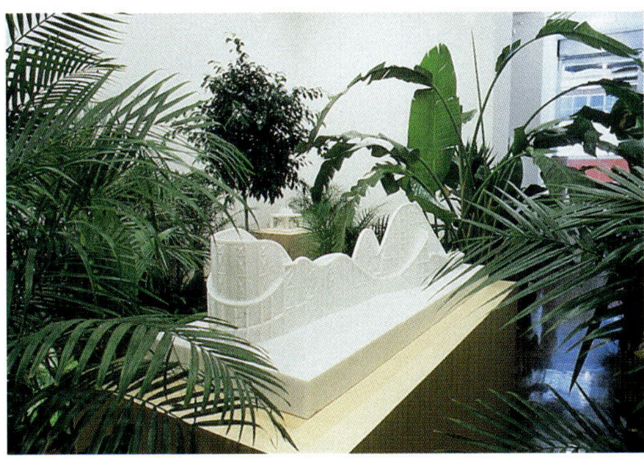

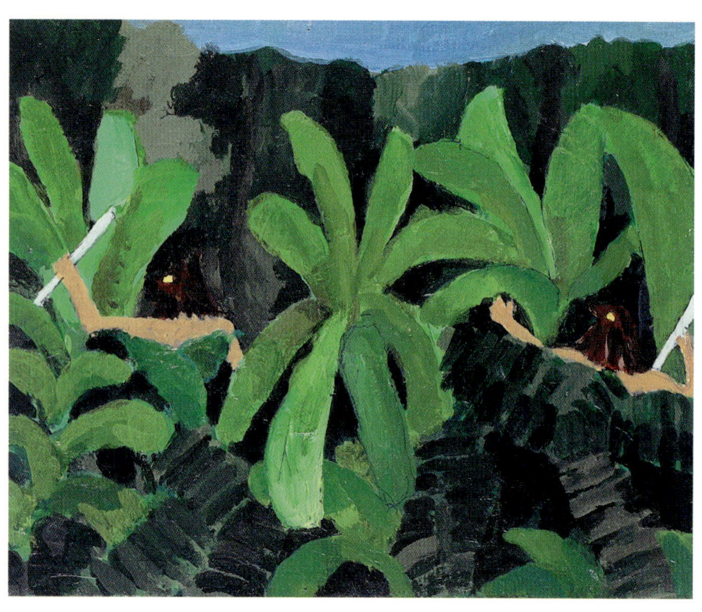

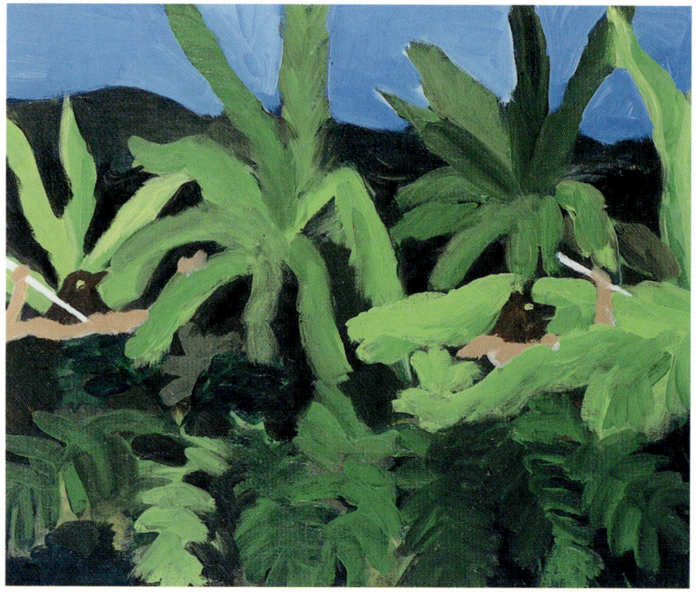

Both paintings entitled *Magic Stick*, 1999, acrylic on canvas, (top) $14^{5}/8$ x 19 inches and (bottom) 15 x 18 inches.

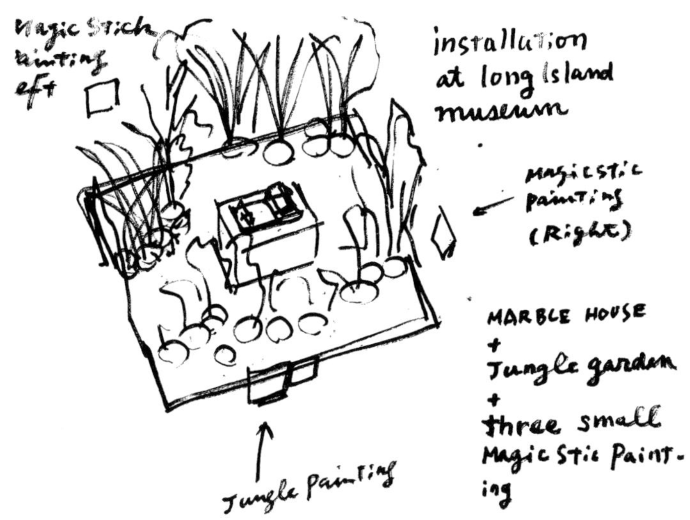

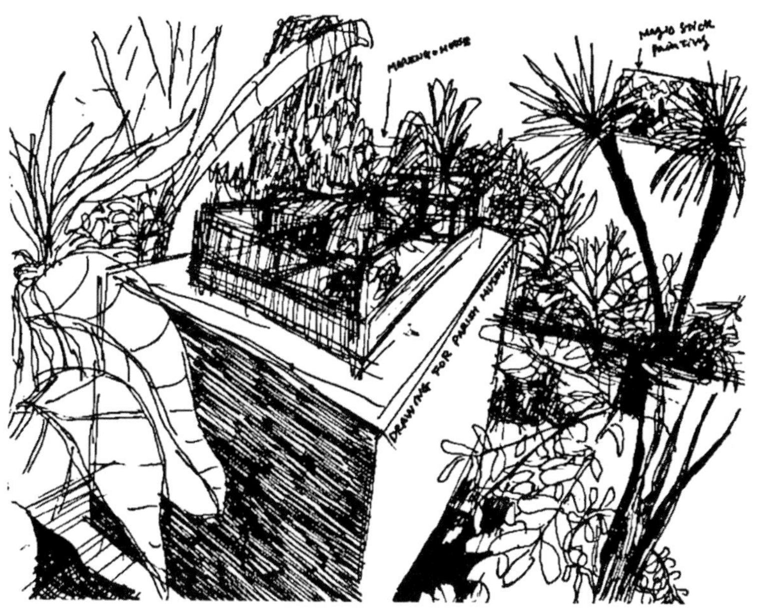

Drawings (sent by facsimile) for Sone's work in progress.

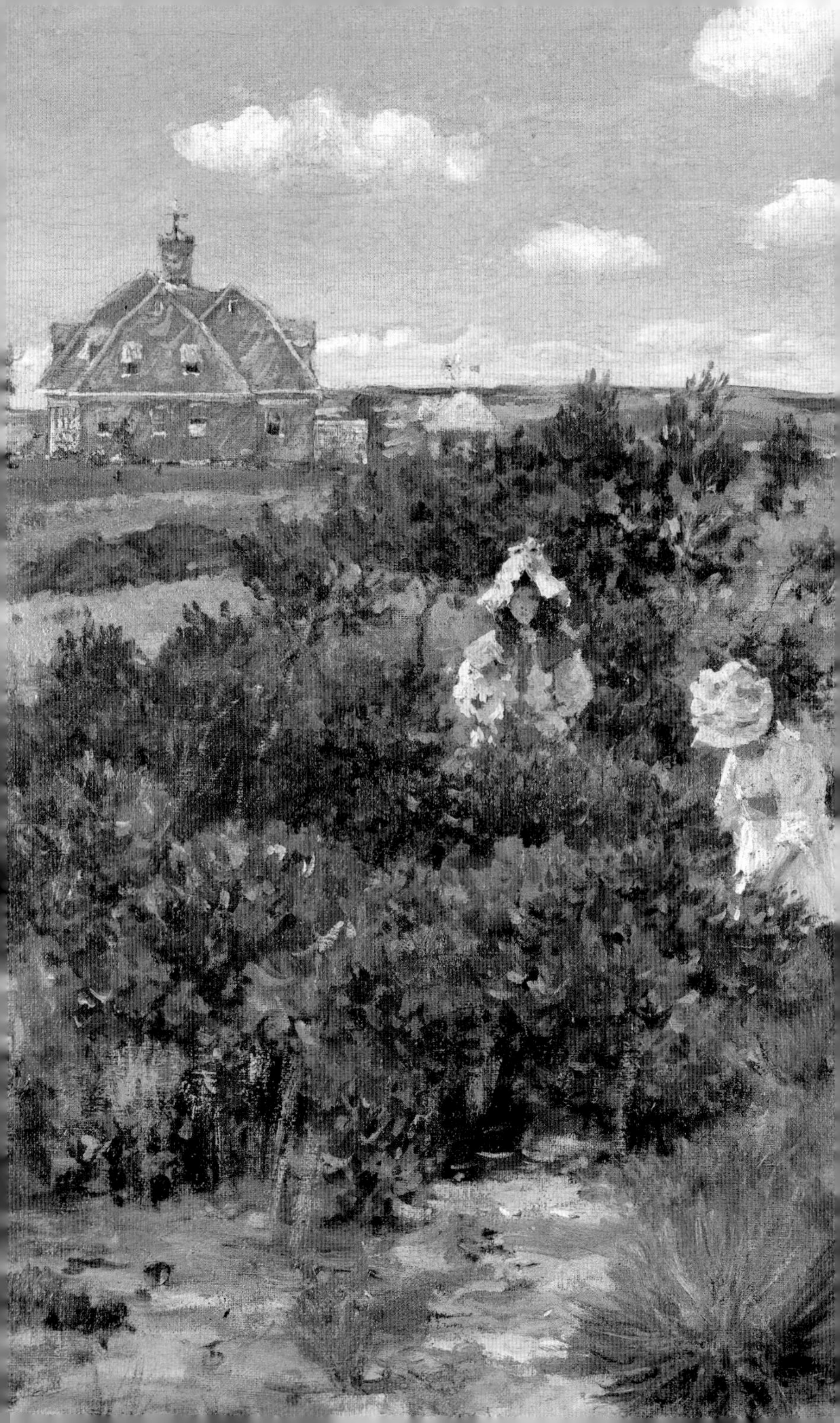

DOSSIER

The term "dossier" is a nod to the artist Joseph Cornell, who considered his collages a form of visual research. His "dossiers" take the form of boxes or files, which could be opened and closed, and continually reelaborated. (An eternal collector, Cornell expressed anxiety over the act of completing any one work.) Each dossier of his, devoted to a specific subject, was filled with materials that could be edited, deleted or augmented, as new finds presented themselves.

The purpose of this dossier on *The Bayberry Bush* is to open the painting to investigation beyond the strictly art historical. All entries are offered as notational, rather than definitive, information on various topics prompted by the painting. The topics touched on are only some of the many possible suggested by Chase's picture. Child rearing, costume, wildlife, real estate, among others, remain to be explored.

There are two kinds of entries: those drawing from published material, for which sources are cited at the end of the entries, and those drawing from interpretations by experts in selected fields who visited the Parrish, looked at *The Bayberry Bush*, and contributed a reading based on, but not necessarily limited to, their area of knowledge. I am extremely grateful to them for their valuable time and insights. —I.S.

TOPICS

ARCHAEOLOGY *mystery fort*

ARCHITECTURE *real estate, Shingle Style, Stanford White*

ARCHIVES *Chase family, photographs,* tableaux vivants

ARTIST *career, human camera, legacy*

BOTANY: DR. STUART LOWRIE *bayberries, gardening, medicine, preservation*

GEOLOGY: DR. STEPHEN LEATHERMAN *beach culture, big trees, moraine*

GEOMORPHOLOGY: DR. ROBERT TURNER *glaciers, sand hills, ticks*

PAINTING *aliases, Mrs. Littlejohn, Mr. Parrish, popularity*

THE SHINNECOCK *colonists, cultural history, the reservation, wampum*

THE SHINNECOCK SUMMER SCHOOL OF ART *Art Village, Chase as teacher, queering, Witch Winnie*

WEATHER: RICHARD HENDRICKSON *clouds, grass, summer, wind*

WHALING: DR. JOHN STRONG *big business, flower pots, Indian whalers*

Page 89: Map of the Shinnecock Hills, showing the Art Village (Copyright F. W. Beers, New York, 1894). Collection Southampton Historical Museum.

Page 90: The William Merritt Chase house today.

Page 91: Chase house, Shinnecock Hills, c. 1908. Cyanotype, $2^1/_2$ x $4^1/_4$ inches. The William Merritt Chase Archives, The Parrish Art Museum, Gift of Mrs. A. Byrd McDowell.

Page 93: Robert, Roland, unidentified woman, and Alice Gerson Chase in front of the Chase house, Shinnecock Hills, 1910. Cyanotype, $2^1/_4$ x $3^1/_4$ inches. The William Merritt Chase Archives, The Parrish Art Museum, Gift of Mrs. A. Byrd McDowell.

Page 94: Alice Gerson Chase, Mary Content, Roland, Robert, Hazel, Helen, Dorothy, Koto, and Alice Dieudonnée, c. 1907. Cyanotype, $2^1/_4$ x $3^1/_2$ inches. The William Merritt Chase Archives, The Parrish Art Museum, Gift of Jackson Chase Storm.

Page 95: Chase in his studio, Shinnecock Hills, c. 1896. Albumen print, $4^5/_8$ x $6^1/_8$ inches. The William Merritt Chase Archives, The Parrish Art Museum, Gift of Jackson Chase Storm.

Page 98: Alice Gerson Chase putting away preserves, Shinnecock Hills, c. 1910. Gelatin silver print, $3^1/_4$ x $5^1/_2$ inches. The William Merritt Chase Archives, The Parrish Art Museum, Gift of Jackson Chase Storm.

Page 101: Mary Content on the old sand road, Shinnecock Hills, c. 1910. Cyanotype, $2^1/_4$ x $3^1/_4$ inches. The William Merritt Chase Archives, The Parrish Art Museum, Gift of Mrs. A. Byrd McDowell.

Page 103: Page from June 1893 *Harper's New Monthly Magazine*, showing Chase's *Shinnecock Indian Girl*, c. 1892 (whereabouts unknown).

Page 105: Reenactment of the landing of colonial settlers in Southampton. Still from Pathé newsreel of the 275th-anniversary celebration of the founding of the Village of Southampton, 1915. Collection Southampton Historical Museum.

Page 107: Shinnecock Summer School of Art prospectus, 1895. The William Merritt Chase Archives, The Parrish Art Museum.

Page 108: Illustration by J. Wells Champney from *Witch Winnie at Shinnecock*, 1894.

Page 109: Chase before his class at the Shinnecock Summer School of Art, c. 1892. Albumen print, $4^3/_8$ x $6^3/_8$ inches. The William Merritt Chase Archives, The Parrish Art Museum, Gift of Jackson Chase Storm.

Page 111: Chase, Mary Content, and Roland, Shinnecock Hills, c. 1905. Cyanotype, $2^1/_4$ x $1^3/_8$ inches, mounted on album page. The William Merritt Chase Archives, The Parrish Art Museum, Gift of Jackson Chase Storm.

Page 112: Chase house, Shinnecock Hills. Cyanotype, printed on penny postcard, $5^1/_2$ x $3^1/_2$ inches. Postmarked September 10, 1909, with note from "Lady Pansies" (Mrs. Chase) to Miss Bessie Fisher, requesting "brown liquid to photograph or rather print with." The William Merritt Chase Archives, The Parrish Art Museum, Gift of Mrs. A. Byrd McDowell.

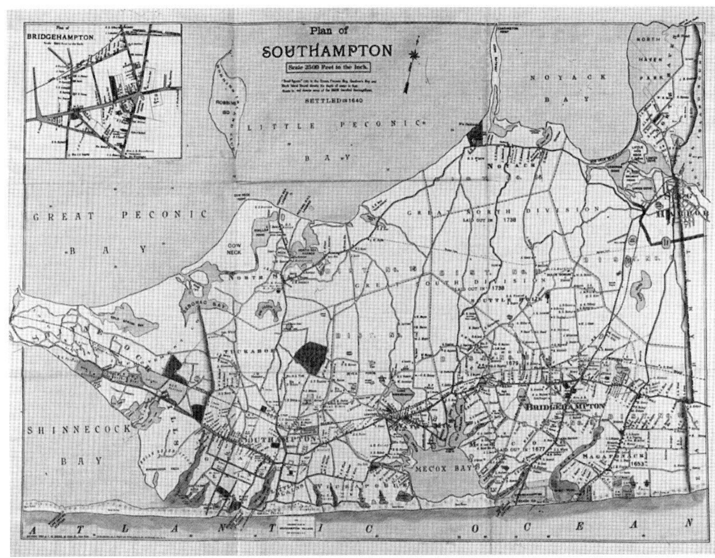

ARCHAEOLOGY

Settlement: Indian villages in the Shinnecock Hills and elsewhere on Long Island were not the large-scale communities typical of New England. Archaeological studies indicate that island Indians set up small homesteads. Their forts featured palisade architecture: walls of tree trunks jammed side by side into trenches. Such forts usually leave distinct archaeological evidence.

Fort or Fiction? In the late 1980s and early 1990s, controversy raged in Suffolk County, which encompasses the setting for *The Bayberry Bush*. At the center of the debate were claims of the remains of an Indian fort in the Shinnecock Hills near Southampton; the presence of these remains would warrant preservation and preclude real estate development. Minor artifacts found on the site, and the geography, led one archaeologist to state that the existence of a fort was almost a certainty.

On the basis of these claims, the county purchased a parcel of the land in question, then enlisted the Suffolk County Archaeological Association to conduct a proper dig. Eventually, none of the distinctive signs of a palisade fort was discovered.

Verdict: There is no proof as yet that the spot where William Merritt Chase's three daughters gathered around the bayberry bush is an important archaeological site. Its value and meaning otherwise are to be seen.

Source: Articles by Dele Olojede in *Newsday* (Nassau/Suffolk County edition), June 9–September 16, 1990.

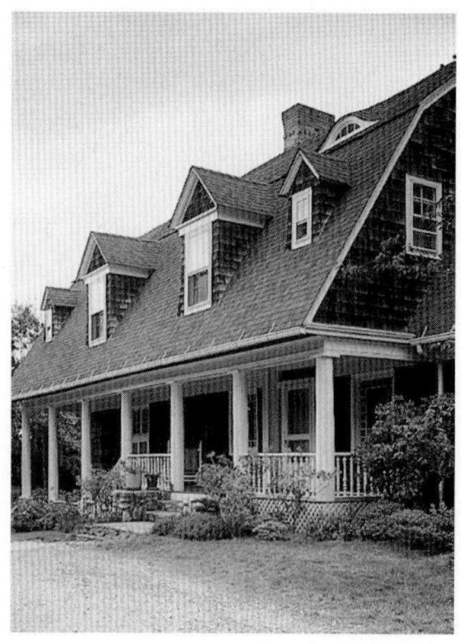

ARCHITECTURE

The Firm: McKim, Mead & White (Charles, William & Stanford) was the most celebrated American architectural enterprise of the Gilded Age. From a pastiche of Old World and classical references, its partners created a New World architecture. Opulent mansions at Newport, Rhode Island, the Boston Public Library, and the original Pennsylvania Station in New York City are some of its best-known constructions.

Among its Long Island works were a Southampton residence for the lawyer and museum founder Samuel Parrish (1889) and the clubhouse for the nation's first country club and organized golf course, in the Shinnecock Hills (1892).

A Freebie: There is no doubt that William Merritt Chase's Shinnecock home was designed by the firm, but there is some question about its commission. No record of payment exists. The rendering for the exterior in the McKim, Mead & White archives predates the opening of the Shinnecock Summer School of Art. There is also no record that Chase ever purchased the property: perhaps it was a perquisite of his teaching job. The house was evidently designed for, but never used by, another Shinnecock Hills resident, Charles Atterbury. When Chase accepted the teaching post, Stanford White presented this design as a favor, off the books. A draftsman was apparently assigned to render the interior, which is relatively modest for the firm.

Masters of Arts: Chase and White were cronies. An anecdote has the pair walking down Fifth Avenue in Manhattan arm in arm: Chase in a

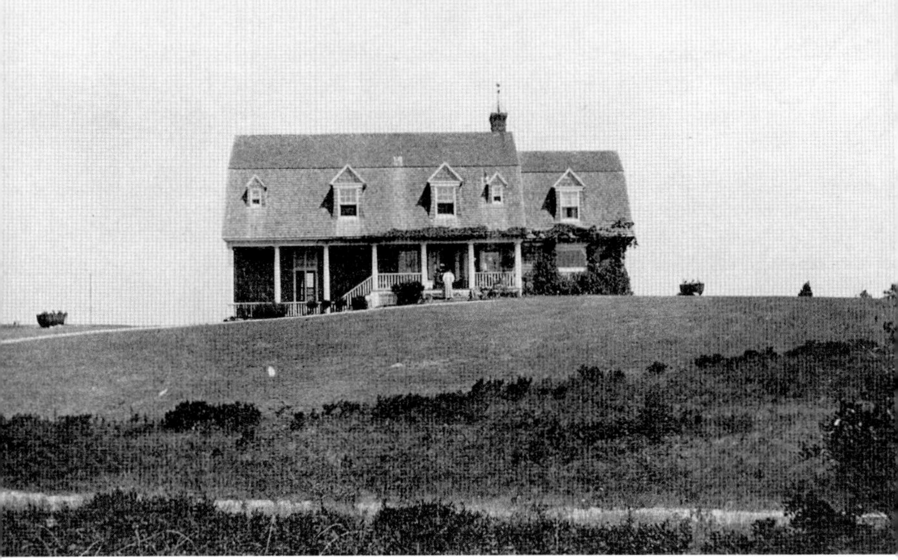

spiffy suit with boutonnière; White with his big mustachios, gesturing wildly; traffic stopping. Both men belonged to the venerable Century Club and the exclusive Tile Club. Members of the latter took their decorative arts seriously: they met weekly for about ten years, starting in 1877, spending the evenings eating, drinking, talking, and painting ceramic tiles.

Wicked Taste: Stanford White was lionized in life, but after he was gunned down by his lover's husband, his reputation fell. (Could such a womanizer make decent buildings?) Chase defended his friend's memory in an interview he gave to the Paris *Herald*:

In my opinion, Stanford White did more to beautify New York and to encourage architectural beauty everywhere in America than any other ten men. . . . Yet, now that his life has ended in a shocking tragedy, America seems likely (if not eager) to forget the debt we owe him. . . . He was a man thoroughly alive, an artist to his finger tips; and he enjoyed life. If it be a fault to admire beautiful women, he possessed that fault. . . . He did not seem to regard it as anything to conceal. Why should he? His instincts were normal. (Quoted in *Biographical Dictionary of American Artists*, 1970, pp. 378–379.)

Bushwhacking: Since Chase's house was not completed until 1892, he spent the summer of 1891 at the new Canoe Place Inn. Still in operation today, it was a part of the commercial development described in an 1890 publication of the Long Island Rail Road:

It is hard to imagine a more desirable location for a summer residence. The land is high, and from this rounded plateau one looks down upon one of the finest marine views on the Atlantic Coast. These "Hills" were purchased by the Long Island Improvement Company, and the finest portion has been transferred to the Shinnecock Inn and Cottage Company, representing prominent New York gentlemen, who have erected a hotel in exact reproduction of an old English inn, and they and other parties have built cottages and made green lawns and gardens where before were sand-heaps and low underbrush. . . . The depot of the Long Island Railroad is in keeping with the style of architecture of the hotels and cottages. (Quoted in *William Merritt Chase: Summers at Shinnecock*, 1987, p. 16.)

All-American: The house is a picture of American architecture. Its main features are a large gambrel roof and a shingled exterior. The gambrel was a standard of McKim, Mead & White's Newport architecture, where it echoed local eighteenth-century structures. In harking back to the seventeenth-century saltbox, the Shingle Style is indigenously American. (Until the architectural historian Vincent Scully dubbed it "Shingle Style," it was called "modern colonial.") The colonial revival came on strong in the United States after the Civil War, when a common heritage could, at least architecturally, unify a rent nation. It was initiated by a group of young architects around 1876, when it was shown to the public at the Centennial Exposition in Philadelphia, and was subsequently popularized by McKim, Mead & White, which made it *the* northeastern coastal architecture of the late 1800s.

Shipshape: The principal attraction in Chase's house was the two-story open volume of the great hall/living room, with its stone fireplace and sweeping staircase. Nautical details in the wood newel posts and column capitals, carved to resemble rope, summon the marine surroundings, and shiny tongue-and-groove board recalls the interior of a yacht. The studio does not appear to have been designed as such. To receive the proper light to paint by, Chase had to add a large northern window to one of the rooms and cover a bank of existing windows with tapestries.

Landmark: The William Merritt Chase house remains in private hands; in the 1970s, it received landmark status from the National Register of Historic Houses.

Sources: D. Scott Atkinson and Nicolai Cikosvky, Jr., *William Merritt Chase: Summers at Shinnecock, 1891–1902* (Washington, DC: National Gallery of Art, 1987). Samuel G. White with Jonathan Wallen, *The Houses of McKim, Mead & White* (New York: Rizzoli, with the Museums at Stony Brook, 1998).

ARCHIVES

Souvenirs: Included in the William Merritt Chase Archives at the Parrish are some one thousand photographs, as well as correspondence, reproductions of Chase's art, publications, and artifacts (such as the artist's paint box and palette, a saltshaker of his, and a self-portrait bowl).

Gifts: The Archives comprise several donations made since 1976, chiefly by Chase's descendants. The collection was solicited by Ronald Pisano, Chase scholar and former Parrish Museum director.

Shutterbug: Family life is the main subject of the photographs. Most were taken probably by the artist's wife, Alice Gerson Chase, who learned photography from Elizabeth Fisher, a close family friend. There are many cyanotypes, those inexpensive blue-toned prints favored by amateurs. For whatever skills Alice lacked as a photographer—the images are often smudged or out of focus—she compensated with enthusiasm. When he was on trips abroad, Chase thanked her for sending pictures of the children and commented on her compositions.

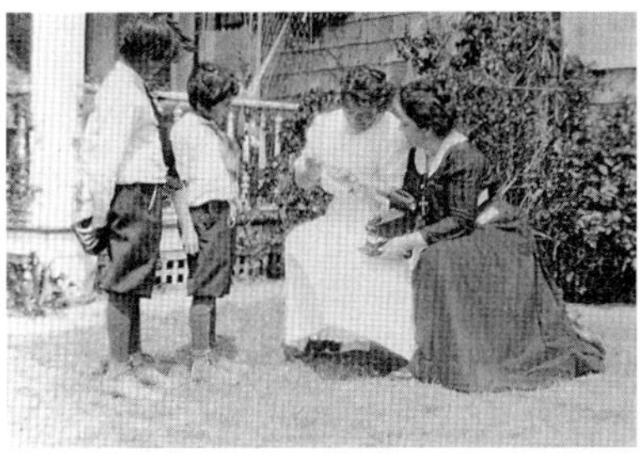

Little Alice: The daughter of well-to-do New Yorkers, Alice Gerson was about fourteen when she met Chase; she formed an instant attachment to him. He was in his early thirties, enjoying a reputation of confirmed bachelorhood. Her devotion won his, and in 1887, when she was twenty, they married. The first of their eight children was born the following day. Photographs show a close, happy family.

Nomenclature: The Chase children, from youngest to oldest, were Mary Content, Roland Dana, Robert Stewart, Helen Velasquez, Hazel Neamaug, Dorothy Brémond, Koto Robertine, and Alice Dieudonnée (nicknamed Cosy). The three girls in *The Bayberry Bush* are most likely Dorothy Brémond (red ribbon); Helen Velasquez (yellow); Alice Dieudonnée (blue).

Exotica: In Chase's day, things Japanese were deemed fashionable and artistic. Photographs show him toting a giant Japanese umbrella around the dunes. Whenever a child was born at Shinnecock, he marked the occasion by flying high a Japanese red paper fish. Hazel

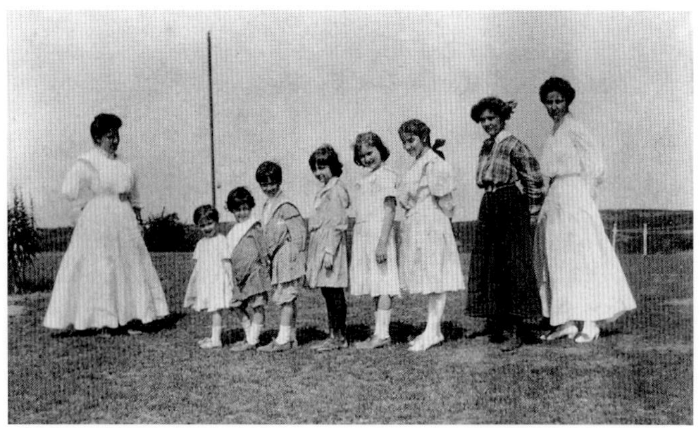

Neamaug was known as "the first white child born on the Shinnecock Hills"; Neamaug supposedly meant "between the two waters"—the Indian name for the Shinnecock Canal.

Dress-up: To judge from the number of photographs of the family posed in costume (in kimonos, in fancy and historic dress, as Indians and Arabs), the Chases loved a good *tableau vivant*. "Living pictures," complete with props, were popular Victorian entertainment. Chase acted out his love of Velázquez by having his daughters dress up as infantas; sometimes they are photographed standing behind ornate picture frames.

Source: Ronald G. Pisano and Alicia Grant Longwell, *Photographs from the William Merritt Chase Archives at The Parrish Art Museum* (Southampton, NY: The Parrish Art Museum, 1992).

ARTIST

William Merritt Chase: Born in Williamsburg, Indiana, November 1, 1849. Died in New York City, October 25, 1916.

American Artist: At the peak of his career, Chase epitomized the successful American artist of the Gilded Age. He trained in Germany, where he mastered an academic style, and after touring Europe, he returned to New York, where he cut an image of sophisticated cosmopolitanism. An impeccable dresser—even in the studio he wore white flannel suits, velvet jackets, eyeglasses on ribbons, a jeweled ring around his cravat—Chase no doubt impressed newly rich Americans insecure of their own cultural identity. Yet his professional persona was reassuringly businesslike; he was the antithesis of the fop aesthete whom Americans associated with the Old World, as personified by, say, Oscar Wilde. Chase's milieu was of like-minded men, including business tycoons, architects, and artists committed to advancing American capitalism in the guise of cultural tradition.

Studio as Department Store: Chase established a studio suited to the new industrial age. Located in the Tenth Street Studio Building in Manhattan (an artists' collective where Chase worked from 1878 through 1895), it was appointed as opulently as a Victorian department store. Full of art reproductions and gewgaws (stuffed polar bear and pink cockatoos, dried devilfish, scarlet Spanish donkey blanket, Italian coat-of-arms, Venetian lamps, Japanese bronzes, Egyptian vases) and watched over by a bust of Voltaire and Chase's two pet Russian borzois, it was designed to cultivate clients, showcase the artist's good taste, and promote sales. And it was widely publicized in the contemporary media. (As a young man, Chase had worked in a family-run department store, where his talent for selling ladies' shoes, he later claimed, served him well in the business of getting his art into exhibitions and obtaining portrait commissions.)

Human Camera: A pre-Warholian art-making machine, Chase was

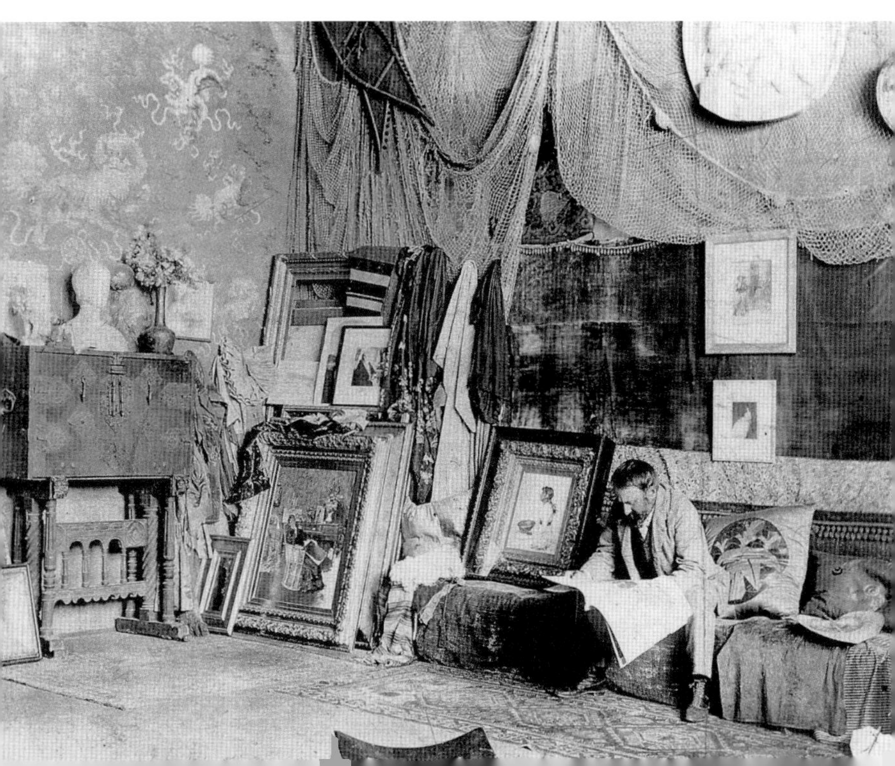

famous in the press for being a "wonderful human camera." He was known to carry around a black paper frame to compose pictures on sight, and to churn out still lifes, landscapes, and portraits. He had a reputation for making anything look good—from a stand of trees in Central Park to a bush on Long Island. Even his paintings of dead fish were prized.

Teaching Machine: Chase was a prodigious teacher, his students numbering in the thousands. He taught at the Art Students League in New York City, and in Philadelphia, Boston, Chicago, and San Francisco. After leaving the Shinnecock school, he conducted summertime teaching tours of Europe.

Hold the Modernism: Chase was affiliated with The Ten, a group of artists associated with American Impressionism, and is considered a chief exponent of that style. He was leery of the French Impressionists, whom he considered too scientific and theoretical—too modern. His approach comes from the Munich school's training in bravura brushwork and trademark dramatic dark palette. These, along with the school's predilection for the seventeenth-century masters Hals and Velázquez, characterize his early work. But by 1880, Chase had perked up his palette to reflect the essential prettiness of contemporary life as he saw it. He called himself a realist.

Legacy: At the time of his death, Chase was honored by the academy and rejected by the avant-garde. In terms of twentieth-century art, his most famous students, including Georgia O'Keeffe, Charles Demuth, Marsden Hartley, and Charles Sheeler, apparently learned how *not* to paint from Chase. Less obvious is the lesson he set by example. Committed to the value of technique, he was conservative but not reactionary. He taught students not to copy him, but to find their own way of seeing and then to stick with it. His was the model of a life passionately devoted to art.

Sources: Sarah Burns, *Inventing the Modern Artist: Art & Culture in Gilded Age America* (New Haven, CT, and London: Yale University Press, 1996). Barbara Dayer Gallati, *William Merritt Chase: Modern American Landscapes, 1886–1890* (New York: Brooklyn Museum of Art, 2000). Ronald G. Pisano, *A Leading Spirit in American Art: William Merritt Chase, 1849–1916* (Seattle: Henry Art Gallery Association, University of Washington, 1983). Katherine Metcalf Roof, *The Life and Art of William Merritt Chase* (1917; repr. New York: Hacker Art Books, 1975).

BOTANY

Report: Dr. Stuart Lowrie visited the Parrish on August 8, 2000; these notes are based on conversation and correspondence that followed.

A botanist by training, with a doctorate from the University of Michigan, Stuart Lowrie is a government relations professional with the Nature Conservancy on Long Island. His work seeks to preserve the plants, animals, and natural communities that represent the diversity of life on earth, by saving the lands and waters they need to survive.

Aliases: Bayberry, or northern bayberry as described in manuals, is known among botanists as *Myrica pensylvanica*. Pollen from this species may cause hay fever.

Mock Cherry: Chase's painting shows two different stages of bayberry growth. The old branches, those sticking up, could be twenty to forty years old. New growth is sprouting at the stumps. In the winter, when temperatures are too low for water to circulate in the plant and maintain its leaves, the bush drops them. Bayberry bark is thin; it grows continuously and smoothly, with conspicuous lenticels, small "holes" that probably allow oxygen access to inner parts of the stems and branches. This characteristic of the bark makes it easy to confuse a bayberry with a young black cherry.

Sex and Berries: There are male and female bushes. In early spring, the males produce catkins, soft, dangly growths that look like pussywillow flowers, filled with pollen, while the females produce an inconspicuous floret. Pollen from the males is carried by wind to the stigmas of the small female flowers, effecting fertilization. By autumn, the berries are mature, with a waxy covering that turns them gray. They are a favorite food item of birds and small mammals, squirrels and chipmunks especially. The berries are used to make candles; they also have medicinal applications.

Bitter Brews and Better Breath: Indians used bayberry (as did and do European-descended herbalists) as an astringent, a stimulant, and a tonic. Among Louisiana Indians, a bayberry tea was given to reduce fever, and in the Southeast, it treated "spongy gums." It was also mixed with other plants in a concoction meant to strengthen gums and whiten teeth.

Myrica has the most effective influence in diseased mucous accumulation of the alimentary canal, which in this morbid soil is an incubator for bronchopulmonic diseases. (Alma Hutchens, *Indian Herbology of North America*, 1969.)

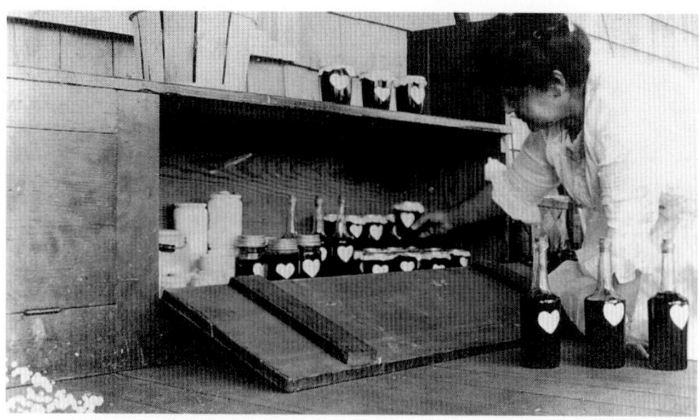

Supporting Roles: In addition to the bayberry bush, Dr. Lowrie identified these plants in Chase's painting:

SWITCHGRASS (*Panicum virgatum*). Shown in fruit and having entered into senescence, the stage in plant life from full maturity to death, characterized by an accumulation of metabolic products, an increase in respiratory rate, and a loss in dry weight, especially in leaves and fruit.

INDIAN GRASS (genus *Sorghastrum*). Also shown in fruit.

LITTLE BLUE STEM (*Schizachyrium scoparium*).

GOLDEN ASTER (genus *Chrysopis*). A likely example is the yellow flower.

EASTERN RED CEDAR (*Juniperus virginiana*).

DUNE GRASS (*Ammophila breviligulata*). *Ammophila* means "sand lover."

Reported Missing: Very common in the dune community is the evergreen or seaside goldenrod (*Solidago sempervirens*), which here is conspicuous by its absence. There should also be more beach plums (genus *Prunis*).

Extinct Pink? There are touches of pink in the dunes. Once characteristic of maritime grasslands, the sandplain gerardia (*Agalinis acuta*) is listed by the United States Fish and Wildlife Service as endangered. Seven of its thirteen populations remaining in the world are found on Long Island, where its flowers once colored entire plains pink in the fall.

Unidentified Life Form: What is that spiky succulent thing in the foreground? It looks like an aloe. Alien to this landscape, perhaps it arrived on the wings of Chase's imagination when he decided some vegetation should fill the patch of dirt in the front of the painting.

Green Thumbs: It is unlikely that the lawn around Chase's house would have been watered or irrigated throughout the summer. It should be brown at this time of year. But painted green does make a more pleasant impression, and it sets the domesticated landscape off from the natural one.

The flowers planted around the house are probably geraniums and marigolds.

Burning Bush: When the hills were still theirs, the Shinnecock burned them regularly, to clear them of parasites (ticks) and open them for hunting, and later (post-contact) to encourage the growth of grass for livestock. Once this practice ended, the landscape changed, according to the natural order of succession. Holly, sumac, scrub oak, beach plum, and serviceberry would grow, then (depending on proximity to the ocean) such trees as oaks and beeches. Eventually, a maritime oak forest could develop here.

Erased from the Face of the Earth: The maritime grassland typified by the Shinnecock landscape is a globally imperiled natural community: few acres of its type are left in the world. The Nature Conservancy is working to restore and preserve one of the best surviving examples, located in Montauk, at the eastern tip of Long Island.

GEOLOGY

Report: Dr. Stephen Leatherman visited the Parrish on May 31, 2000; these notes are based on a tape recording of his observations.

Dr. Leatherman, known to some as "Dr. Beach," is famous for his yearly reports on the country's top beaches. He directs the National Hurricane Center in Miami, and has collaborated with the Eastern Long Island Coastal Conservation Alliance on a three-year study of changes to local beachfronts.

Moraine Terrain: "We're looking at an area that's pretty sandy, with some rocks. This is what you would expect from moraine: sediments, materials of different sizes, pushed in front of a glacier, as if by a bulldozer. The entire backbone of Long Island is moraine."

Cape Cod Equals Long Island? The two regions have similar geological pasts, and were settled by the same kinds of people (farmers, fishermen), with similar ideas about the land. "I'm not an expert here, because I haven't done the historical work. But I've done it for Cape Cod, and the similarity strongly suggests that the Shinnecock Hills were once covered with big trees." (Since the 1970s, Leatherman has researched and published on the natural history of Cape Cod.)

Accounts by early settlers of Cape Cod describe forests fit to ride a horse through, meaning a good canopy, no scrub. Hardwood trees were everywhere, even in sandy soil. If you visit those sites on the Cape today, you'll see even less vegetation than appears in *The Bayberry Bush*.

Natural Succession: The first plants to take hold on the moraine would have been shrubs. Then pine trees, and sometimes cedars. Finally the hardwoods, which would have blocked out the sun, would come to dominate the landscape.

Stumps: Southampton is the earliest settlement in New York State. Any hardwood forests would have been clear-cut by colonists needing timber for fuel and for construction of buildings and boats. The stumps would have vanished long ago.

On the Beach: When did people start coming to Long Island for its littoral amenities? Beach culture began in England around 1880 and didn't really take off in the United States until later. Chase's era saw the growth of leisure culture, with people building summer homes and cottages, especially by lakes and other bodies of water. In his day, people in Southampton would have been more apt to swim in the bay—not as high-quality an experience as in the ocean. Bay water is not as refreshingly cool, and it has plenty of seaweed. The ocean has clearer, more buoyant water and, of course, waves.

The Rise of the Hamptons: The New Jersey shore and Coney Island were the original popular meccas of New York City beach culture. On Long Island, the first area to be developed was Quogue, which was as far as you could get from the city on a tank of gas in 1930. Westhampton Beach boasted the most expensive real estate until the 1938 hurricane devastated it. Westhampton was succeeded by Southampton, which experienced major development in the 1960s. More recently, East Hampton has been attracting the rich and famous; the average cost of a home there is $800,000. To Dr. Beach, however, "Southampton remains the prominent cultural center of Long Island. It has a fascinating history."

GEOMORPHOLOGY

Report: Dr. Robert Turner is quoted from correspondence of May 2000.

Coastal geologist Robert Turner, Ph.D., has been a professor of natural sciences at Southampton College since 1999. He has written extensively on beach morphologies and morpho-

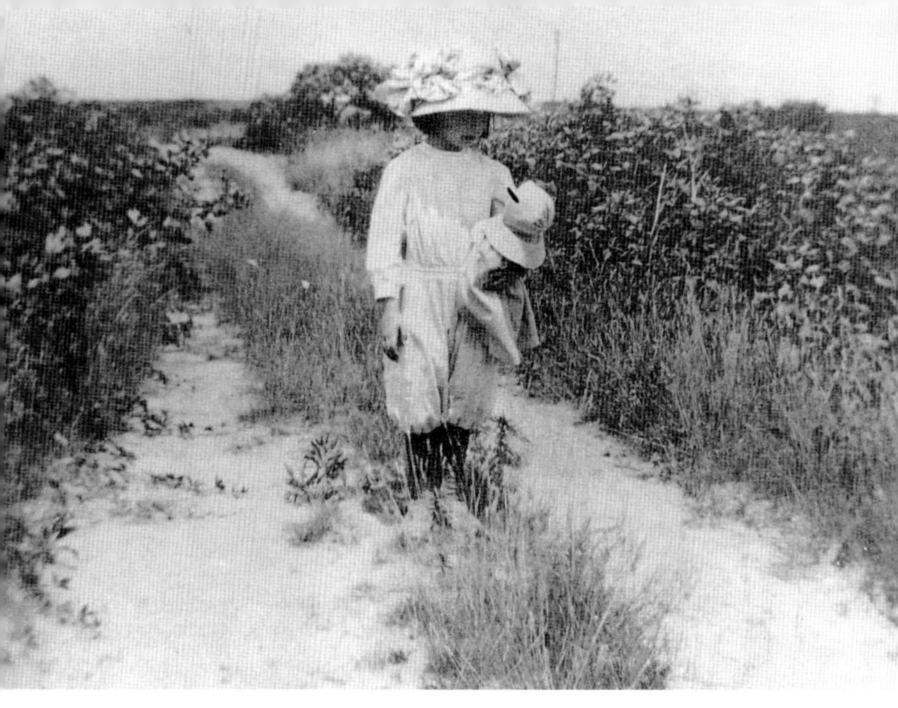

dynamics. His upcoming fieldwork will focus on the geophysical and biochemical impacts of opening an inlet to Sagaponack Lake. Dr. Turner's assessment is based on, in his words, "general geomorphological principles, vague scuttlebutt, and imagination."

First Impression: "Somebody better check those girls for ticks when they come back inside."

Glacial History: "Certainly the geomorphology and plant assemblage are a legacy of the glacial history of Long Island. Or to be somewhat more poetic, the nature of the landscape is born of ice, wind, and fire. It may look very calm and peaceful, but it is actually a rather harsh environment."

Sensuous Hills: "Between approximately 22,000 and 20,000 years ago, glacial ice extended from the North Pole down to the vicinity of the Shinnecock Hills. While the snout of the continental glacier was parked here, it shed enormous amounts of sediment. The finer-grained silts and clays were carried away by glacial meltwater, leaving behind large deposits of sand and gravel. Glacial meltwater and strong winds re-deposited the sand into the sensuous hills that constitute the unique topography."

Glacial Heritage: "That the hills are composed predominantly of sand, with little silt or clay, results in a land surface which is very poor in organic constituents and very permeable to rain. The low nutrient content of the 'soil' and its inability to retain water, along with the persistent winds, make the landscape very dry, unsuitable for farming, and prone to periodic brushfires. These factors, along with harvesting of the pine trees by English settlers, account for the dominance of hardy grasses and the occasional shrub. Such barren sandy land was historically considered useless except to those with an aesthetic appreciation for open spaces, big sky, and unaltered nature. As a consequence, land with this glacial heritage has been some of the last to get developed."

Crunchy Beauty, Thirsty Girls: "The bright, crunchy, forbidding beauty of these sand hills invites only short visitations. . . . That makes the supposed exploration of the area by these girls all the more intrepid. They are undoubtedly getting scratched up and thirsty. That the girl on the right is sitting down seems to indicate that she has had it with poking around in this scruffy wilderness. If that bayberry bush is the most interesting thing this landscape has to offer, well, she'll just have a seat and wait for her friends to get tired of their sport. I think it likely that they were attracted to this spot by the presence of William Merritt Chase and are not avid explorers of the property. The landscape is static, and so are they."

***Tableau Vivant*:** "I think I hear the brunette saying, 'Poppa, I liked it better when you painted the beach." Miss Redbow looks ready to go back to the house and would probably be pleased to know that this land will eventually be transformed into a fairway or lawn."

Alien Life Forms: "The inclusion of these brightly colored children into the landscape, like alien flowers, really emphasizes the harsh peacefulness of the environment. They have been subdued by it. Here is a place where human activity, even the irrepressible energy of young girls, is incongruous. As such, it is a perfect retreat for the contemplative artist or harried adult. Save the Shinnecock Hills!"

Conservation: The site of *The Bayberry Bush* has been transformed by development and landscaping; the Chase house is now barely visible from a distance. "At many home sites, the soil has been enhanced with topsoil, fertilizers, and compost. Also, fires have been discouraged, allowing a buildup of organic matter and succession of other plant types. Certain areas have been preserved. There's a nature preserve near Southampton College operated by the Nature Conservancy."

PAINTING

Group Identity: *The Bayberry Bush* falls into the larger group of works by Chase known as the Shinnecock paintings. Like most of the others, it is undated. The attribution to 1895 or thereabouts is based on the sizes and apparent ages of the artist's daughters depicted.

Aliases: The picture has been exhibited and published under several other titles, including *Chase Homestead, Shinnecock Hills; Shinnecock Landscape;* and *The Big Bayberry Bush*.

Provenance: The Parrish received the picture in 1956 and accepted it into the collection in 1961 as part of a larger gift from Mrs. Robert M. Littlejohn. She had purchased the painting in the 1950s from one of Chase's daughters, Helen Chase Storm, for $500.

Golf and Art: The museum's founder, Samuel Longstreth Parrish, did not collect contemporary art, but he did donate the land on which both the Shinnecock Summer School and Chase's home were built. Considered the First Citizen of Southampton, he was among the businessmen and professionals who developed the area by investing in the nation's first country club and golf course. (An avid golfer, Parrish wrote a treatise on

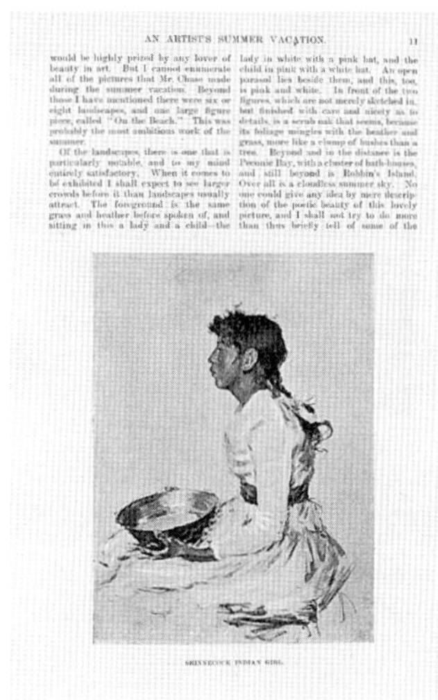

AN ARTIST'S SUMMER VACATION. 11

would be highly prized by any lover of beauty in art. But I cannot enumerate all of the pictures that Mr. Chase made during the summer vacation. Beyond those I have mentioned there were six or eight landscapes, and one large figure piece, called "On the Beach." This was probably the most ambitious work of the summer.

Of the landscapes, there is one that is particularly notable, and to my mind entirely satisfactory. When it comes to be exhibited I shall expect to see larger crowds before it than landscapes usually attract. The foreground is the same grass and heather before spoken of, and sitting in this a lady and a child—the lady in white with a pink hat, and the child in pink with a white hat. An open parasol lies beside them, and this, too, is pink and white. In front of the two figures, which are not merely sketched in, but finished with care and nicety as to details, is a scrub oak that seems, because its foliage mingles with the heather and grass, more like a clump of bushes than a tree. Beyond and in the distance is the Peconic Bay, with a cluster of bath-houses, and still beyond is Robbin's Island. Over all is a cloudless summer sky. No one could give any idea by mere description of the poetic beauty of this lovely picture, and I shall not try to do more than thus briefly tell of some of the

SHINNECOCK INDIAN GIRL.

the sport.) In 1896, he proposed that the new resort have an art museum, which would display his own collection of Renaissance art and copies of classical objects, and only a year later it opened, in an Italianate building designed by Grosvenor Atterbury. Following his death in 1932, Parrish's estate donated the museum to the Village of Southampton.

Local Pride: When Mrs. Robert Littlejohn became president of the museum board in the 1950s, she determined to turn the Parrish from a quaint summertime distraction into a year-round operation. She campaigned for improvement to the building (Atterbury's edifice had crumbled somewhat since Parrish's death) and encouraged the acquisition of works by artists associated with eastern Long Island, in particular William Merritt Chase, whose work she collected in depth.

Chase Bonanza: In 1961, when Mrs. Littlejohn died, her gift to the museum included thirty-one paintings by Chase. Subsequent acquisitions and the development of the Chase Archives make him a focus for the museum. A fund-raising campaign in 1976 centered around a Chase exhibition held at the Knoedler gallery in New York City; proceeds from an uncharacteristic two-dollar admission fee benefited the museum.

Another important figure in the collection is Fairfield Porter (1907–1975); in 1981, his wife, Anne, donated nearly two hundred works.

Poster Child: Although it has yet to travel globally, *The Bayberry Bush* has been exhibited across the United States. It has been included in every major Chase exhibition and is the most frequently requested work in the Parrish collection for loan and reproduction. The museum uses the image for notecards, posters, and membership brochures. It has graced the cover of *American Psychologist* (1997), illustrated an article (about summertime in Rhode Island, however) in *The Christian Science Monitor* (1992), and appeared as a centerfold in the journal of the National Retired Teachers Association (1980).

What's Not to Love? Even without any knowledge of its historic or institutional importance, this picture has popular appeal. It is painted in a style that accords with the museum wisdom "Hang an Impressionist picture, and the people will come." What's more, it packs the sentiment of Victorian childhood, the welcome of a drop-dead summer house, and splendid holiday weather.

Sources: Donna De Salvo, *Past Imperfect: A Museum Looks at Itself* (Southampton, NY: The Parrish Art Museum, 1993). *The Parrish Art Museum: A History of Its Collections and Building* (brochure), n.d.

THE SHINNECOCK

First Contact: Shinnecock culture can be dated to Paleo-Indian times (7,000–3,500 B.C.), and it still exists today. The Shinnecock were among the first indigenous groups to have contact with Europeans, who were impressed by their power, and their wampum industry. An early historian referred to them as "the greatest tribe."

Cash and Corn: In 1627, a colonist described the eastern end of Long Island and its inhabitants thus: "It has several creeks and bays, where

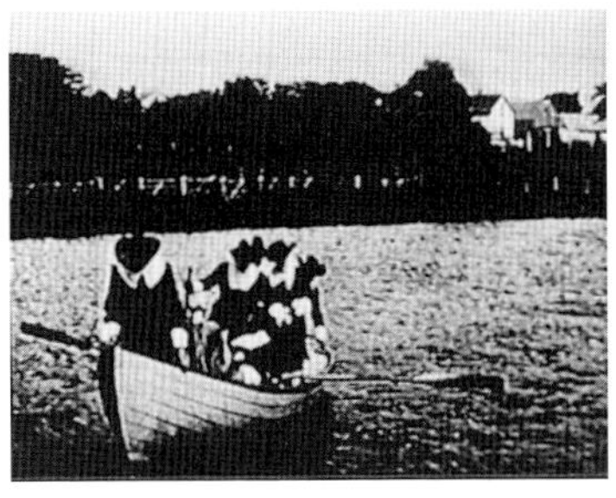

many savages dwell who support themselves by planting maize and making sewan [wampum], and who are called Souwenox and Sinnecox."

Pockets Full of Dough: The Shinnecock may have manufactured wampum near the site depicted in *The Bayberry Bush*. This form of currency was made by grinding down the local Quogue shells, heavy white clamshells streaked purple on the interior. In colonial times, wampum was used by both Europeans and Indians. With European settlers having their own respective mother-country currencies, monetary transactions were bound to have been time-consuming.

Burning Tension: In early colonial days, the Shinnecock burned Southampton homes as a protest to the "usual scenario: their land was 'sold' to colonists for a pittance while they were entertained with gallons of rum; large tracts of their land were taken . . . they were forbidden access to their usual subsistence of gathering ground nuts [and] trapping" (Gaynell Stone, introduction, *The Shinnecock Indians*, p. 1).

Special Sightline: Indian oral tradition underlines the significance of the Shinnecock Hills. Here one could stand and at once see both waters: the Atlantic Ocean and the Great Peconic Bay.

A Little Waxing, a Lot of Waning: In 1703, portions of the Shinnecock Hills that had been appropriated from them, including the terrain of *The Bayberry Bush*, were returned in a concession to the Indians.

In 1859, to make way for the Long Island Rail Road, a thousand-year lease was revamped to favor the interests of local developers, and a major portion of the Hills was taken from the Shinnecock. They were left with essentially the eight hundred acres of today's Shinnecock Reservation.

According to Elizabeth Haile, a resident of the reservation, "The land in the picture by Chase never belonged to Mr. Parrish. He leased it and then he sold it. He owned it because he stole it. This is not a hidden fact."

Mysteries: The authenticity of the document on which the Shinnecock ostensibly approved the amended lease has been questioned. Signatures appear to have been forged. The mystery is compounded by the fact that records kept by the tribal trustees from the time of the transaction have vanished. Furthermore, the 1859 decision was not made with the approval of Congress in Washington, and without that approval, it could be declared void.

Spring Fling: The Shinnecock Hills may have been the setting for an outdoor celebration similar to one documented as held by the Montauk Indians around 1850. A mix of Indian and Christian rituals, it was meant to welcome spring.

Artists and Indians: Chase negotiated with tribal trustees so that students could sketch on the Shinnecock Reservation and use the sailboat dock located on reservation property. Students were charged to sketch Indians; those who attempted to sketch for free risked having their easels confiscated. Some Shinnecock, including one John Thompson, worked for Chase; Shinnecock women took in laundry from the school. Those crisp white frocks that the Chase girls wear in the painting may have been washed by their hands.

Essence of Bayberry: When artist David Bunn Martine looks at *The Bayberry Bush*, he sees "the essence of a time gone by." "I don't know if it was people in general, or just the people who were attracted to my great-grandfather, but it seems like people were more down-to-earth at that time." As a professional guide and hunter from the Shinnecock Reservation, Martine's great-grandfather was in demand among the moneyed elite of Southampton. In his day, duck hunting was a big sport (and business) on Long Island, and it was also the period of the Victorian naturalist. Hence Martine's vision of the Shinnecock Hills as a place where people from opposite sides of privilege convened in the beauty and quiet of open space.

Beyond the Bayberry Bush: Today the Shinnecock are seeking to halt development of sixty-two acres of woodland outside Southampton. They are also trying to reclaim disputed lands, including the entire Shinnecock Hills.

Sources: Charlie LeDuff, "Insular Tribe of the Hamptons Struggles for a Political Voice," *The New York Times*, July 17, 2000, pp. B1, B6. Gaynell Stone, ed., *The Shinnecock Indians: A Culture History* (Stony Brook, New York: Suffolk County Archaeological Association, 1983).

THE SHINNECOCK SUMMER SCHOOL OF ART

Summer Job: During the months William Merritt Chase lived on Long Island, he taught at the Shinnecock Summer School of Art. He conducted a criticism every Monday and led an outdoor painting session on Tuesdays. Once a month he gave a public talk. Otherwise, he was free to do his own work, at a remove from the school's daily life and administration.

The Shinnecock School, one of the first outdoor painting academies in the nation, was founded in 1891, under Chase's direction. It flourished until 1902, when he stopped teaching there. An 1897 prospectus for the school promised "the richest material for the artist in the way of old fences, tangles of rushes, and picturesque boats," in addition to local color: "By special permission, students are allowed to sketch on the Indian Reservation." Not to mention the water: "It has been analyzed and pronounced perfectly pure."

Founding Mothers: The school was initiated by Mrs. William Hoyt, an amateur painter, benefactress, and summer resident of the Shinnecock Hills. Having traveled extensively in Europe, she decided that the United States needed its own version of the French Barbizon:

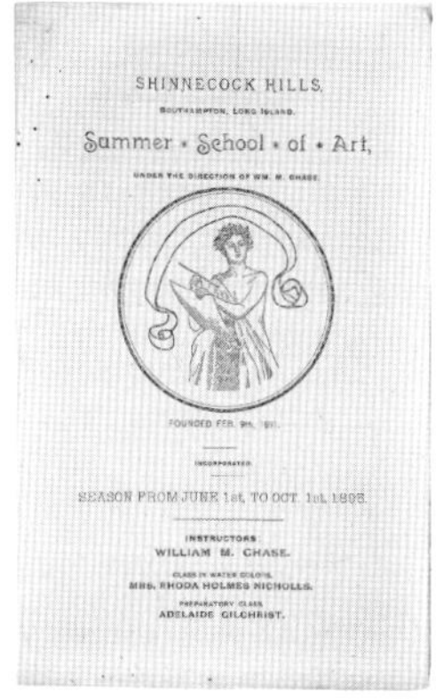
SHINNECOCK HILLS,
SOUTHAMPTON, LONG ISLAND.
Summer • School • of • Art,
UNDER THE DIRECTION OF WM. M. CHASE.
FOUNDED FEB. 9th,
INCORPORATED
SEASON FROM JUNE 1st, TO OCT. 1st,
INSTRUCTORS
WILLIAM M. CHASE.
CLASS IN WATER COLORS,
MRS. RHODA HOLMES NICHOLLS.
PREPARATORY CLASS
ADELAIDE GILCHRIST.

a place for artists to work outside the confines of the studio. Together with Mrs. Henry Porter, Hoyt persuaded leading citizen Samuel Parrish to donate land for the school and invited Chase to teach.

Art Village: The school was located at Art Village, about three miles down the slope from the site of *The Bayberry Bush*. It offered a studio for use on rainy days, a large room for critiques, a supply storage, a dormitory and dining room, and a group of small houses.

Art Village is still known by this name; the original buildings, now reconfigured, are private residences.

Student Body: The classes were made up of more women than men. As many as one hundred students attended each summer, coming from all over the country and even from abroad. Among the more distinguished alumni were the illustrators Howard Chandler

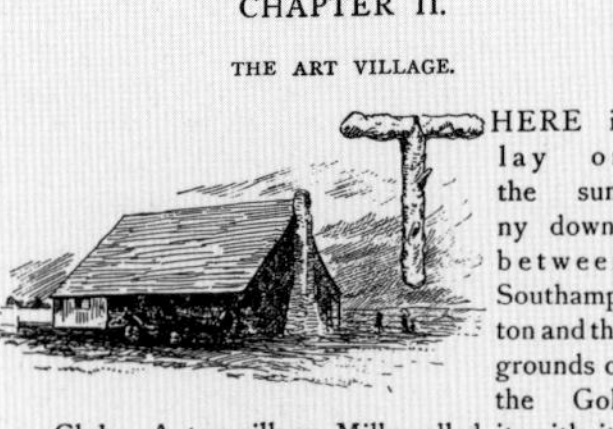
CHAPTER II.

THE ART VILLAGE.

THERE it lay on the sunny downs between Southampton and the grounds of the Golf Club. A toy village Milly called it, with its handful of tiny cottages grouped about the great studio and separated from each other

Christy and Rockwell Kent; the architect John Russell Pope; and the National Academicians Lydia and Ellen Emmett. Lydia eventually joined the staff and taught classes for children.

Monday-Morning Crits: Students assembled with their week's work for a critique by Chase. He was known to be methodical and generous, and would address students individually. A special easel was devised to expedite the process: while one student's work was discussed on one side, the next student would set up on the opposite side of the easel, which would rotate in turn. Sample remarks from the master:

The streaked appearance that we see in the work of the Impressionists is to convey the idea that the air vibrates, that we see through it like a screen, but most of them overdo it.

Don't use too much turpentine. Try a little oil with it.

Too much "chic," Miss W—

Queering: Chase liked to inspire his students with competition. For his "queering" contest, they were asked to compose a picture as awkwardly as possible, then make the image work despite itself. The most successful "queer" would win a drawing by Chase.

Good PR: Some critiques were open to the public, whose noisy commentary turned sessions into a spectacle sport. The public was invited also to lectures and receptions given by Chase. At the end of the season, he would select representative student work for an exhibition at the school; the show would sometimes travel.

Witch Winnie: Elizabeth W. Champney set one of her Witch Winnie books for adolescents at Chase's school. *Witch Winnie at Shinnecock* (New York: Dodd, Mead, 1894), described the Art Village:

There it lay on the sunny downs between Southampton and the grounds of the Golf Club. A toy village Milly called it, with its handful of tiny cottages grouped about the great studio. . . . Tiny cabins with almost an affectation of rusticity in their unpainted rough exteriors, slightly put together but clean and new, and each with its rough fireplace, its irregular windows, its cosey piazza, and its odd corners which differentiated it from its neighbours and gave scope

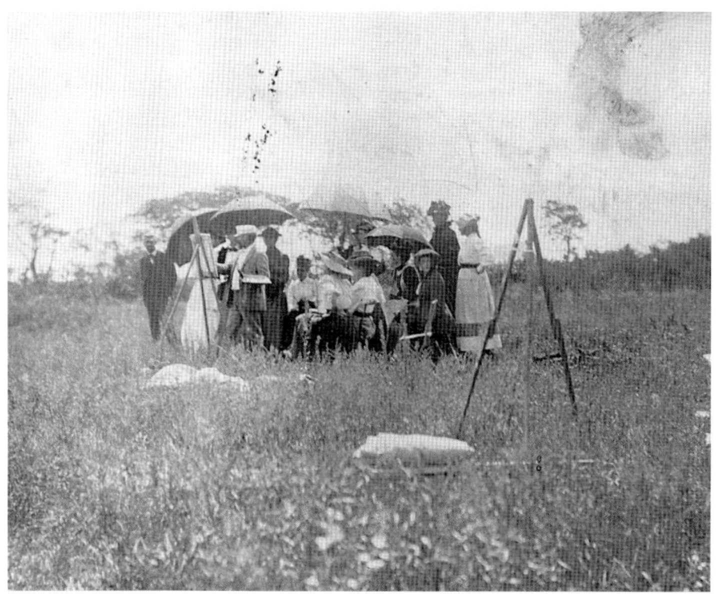

to the individual decorative fancy of its occupants. (p. 17)

And weekly criticisms:

These were frequently witty and entertaining, and the sea-side loungers, swamped by that ennui which is the backwater of the soul . . . were glad to have their torpid natures stirred by the sight of enthusiasm in others. It was almost as cruel as the study of vivisection. . . . The studio was partially filled when they entered. On two sides rows of camp chairs were ranged, and there was a buzz of light chit-chat which told that the master had not yet arrived. . . .

The young lady referred to as Violet, who had boasted that she could adopt the mannerism of the school without being really in sympathy with it, was speedily unmasked. (pp. 23, 28)

As well as the Shinnecock:

And the people! . . . This tribe of Indians, with its admixture of African race, suggested various Oriental types of the picturesque varieties. They were gipsies, Moors, Arabs, Soudanese, Syrians, Egyptians, Turks, or Hindoos, as you pleased to imagine and costume them. . . . Some . . . were available as models, others looked upon the invasion of artists with distrust and hatred. This was particularly the case with the young men, whose instinctive suspicions and jealousy could not be overcome with golden bribes. (p. 68)

Witch Parties: The students diverted themselves and the Chases by staging pageants (a grand procession once met Mrs. Chase at the train), witch parties (held around a steaming cauldron; at one fête, a student emerged from the grass dressed as a sea serpent), dances, cakewalks, *tableaux vivants,* charades, minstrel shows, and even a production of Gilbert and Sullivan's *The Mikado*.

Sources: John H. Morice, "The First Out-of-Door Art School in the United States (Parts I and II)," *The Southampton Press*, November 22, 1946. June L. Ness, "William Merritt Chase and the Shinnecock Summer Art School," *Archives of American Art Journal*, 13, no. 3 (1973), pp. 8–12.

WEATHER

Report: Richard Hendrickson visited the Parrish on June 1, 2000; these notes are based on a tape recording of his observations.

Since 1931, Mr. Hendrickson has been providing the National Weather Service with daily local reports for eastern Long Island. His work is voluntary; "this is the service I do for my country," he says. A retired farmer, Hendrickson is writing a book about his experiences growing up on a poultry and dairy farm. On the day of his visit, he presented the museum staff with a copy of his 1996 book Winds of the Fish's Tail. *This illustrated volume, which takes its title from Walt Whitman's description of Long Island, offers accounts of the weather and its impact on the region.*

Current Conditions: "The picture before me was painted between late August and early September. I am sure the man never painted that nice painting in one day. You have beautiful September clouds. And yet the vegetation—the dull green of the bayberry bush, the dried Shinnecock Hills (nothing but sand, really)—shows late August."

Wind: The wind is coming from the water, as indicated by the weathervane on the pump house, which points south-southwest.

Green: Its warm bright color indicates that the lawn was put in on top of sod ("don't know how deep") that was brought in and irrigated.

The wavy ridges, typical of the Shinnecock Hills, are covered with grass faded to a light color by summertime. Down in the ridges, where soil accumulates, there's some vegetation. The stronger, more vigorous bushes are still showing green.

The Bayberry Bush: The tallest branches have been rubbed bare, possibly by deer. The low branches are new shoots, young growth. Bayberries look like this from early

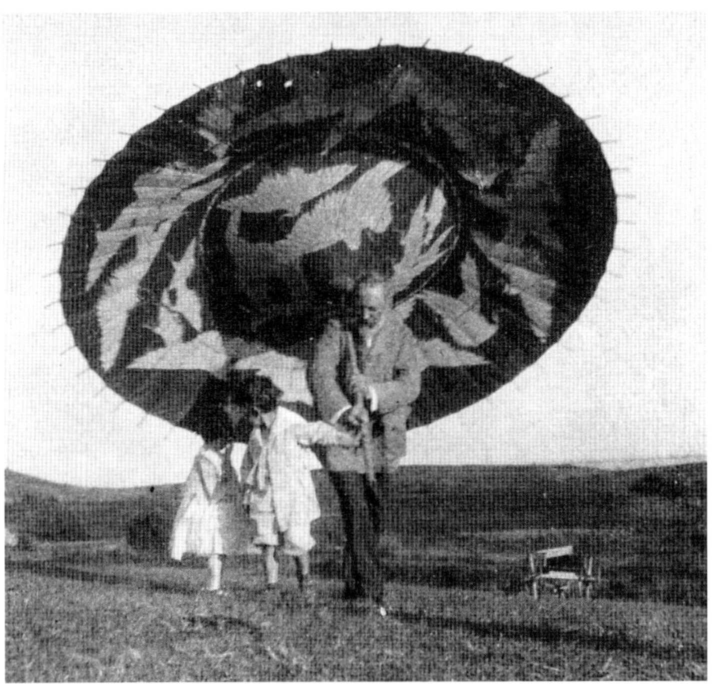

September until somebody picks them or birds eat them. The girls are picking them—an activity that at one time could have been illegal.

Forbidden Fruit: Bayberries are small, about the size of a BB, and white in color. When boiled in a pot of water, they yield a fragrant wax that makes a fine candle (and ruins the pot for cooking). During colonial times, the bushes were far more plentiful than they are today; they were denuded by settlers, and a law was passed regulating when the berries could be picked.

Forecast: "Clear blue skies will remain that way for another day and a half. Clouds will start coming in from the east-northeast—you can see signs already in the distance—bringing darker skies and then rain. Weather holds for three or four days at a stretch."

Recap: "The picture as a whole has the climate and conditions of both August and September. I would put a date of the second week of September on it."

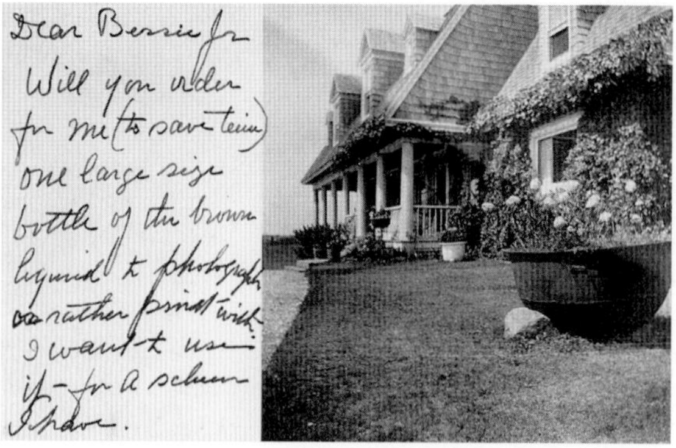

WHALING

Do you see a dark object by the drive to the left of the house in the painting? It's a giant iron kettle of the sort whalers once used for rendering blubber. Outside the Chase home, it has become a decorative planter. In photographs of the house from the Archives, one clearly sees the kettle, and a twin vessel, full of flowers. Following are details about the industry these pots once served.

Report: Dr. John Strong visited the Parrish on August 8, 2000. These notes are from our conversation that day and a later one.

Dr. Strong is professor emeritus of history and American studies at Southampton College.

Big Business: Whale was the first cash crop of eastern Long Island, part of a major industry driven by the market for whale oil, which was used as a lighting fuel. Once rendered, the oil would be transferred to barrels for shipment to Boston and points beyond.

Midnight Oil: The beaches would be dotted with giant iron kettles (also called furnaces). When a whale was brought to shore, the kettles would be heated over fires that would burn for days, while tons of blubber were carved and melted into whale oil. The changing tide would roll the carcasses and facilitate carving.

Colonial Contracts: The early industry was organized by white companies, which hired Indian labor. Crews of twelve would man two boats: on each, four to row, one to steer the rudder, and one harpooner. All earned the same wage, regardless of skill. Whaling season lasted from November to April.

Indian Ceremony: In precolonial times, the Shinnecock did not go out on open sea to hunt. If a whale entered the bay or washed up onshore, it would be butchered. Some Indian religious ceremonies involved the whale's fins or tail. Colonial contracts might designate that these parts of any capture go to the whalers.

Which Whales: The first to be hunted were dubbed right whales, simply enough because they were the right ones to hunt. They fed close to the surface and were easy to approach by boat. After these had been hunted to near-extinction, by the early eighteenth century, whalers had to expand their territory. The industry changed radically: boats would be out for years at a stretch; crews were mainly white. The kettles that had dotted the beaches were moved on board; many whalers burned to death at sea.

Tragic Tale: The history of whaling on eastern Long Island includes one of the most tragic events in local chronicles: the wreck of the British cargo ship *Circassian*. On December 11, 1876, during a storm, as the vessel made its way from Liverpool to New York, it ran aground between Bridgehampton and Southampton, some four hundred yards offshore. The crew was rescued and a new crew assembled to unload the cargo (the bill of lading listed Bath brick, ash, lime, old rags, gelatin, and "100 cases of sauce"). This group drew heavily from the Shinnecock community—experienced seamen, many of them whalers. While work progressed, women and children watched from shore. Just as the unloading was ending, on December 29, another storm hit, the most violent in living memory, and the crew was trapped on board. On land, a rescue crew, families, and neighbors could only watch helplessly as water cleaved the ship in two and men who had lashed themselves to the deck were ripped out to sea. Twenty-eight of the thirty-two on board died.

The toll on the Shinnecock was devastating: the income-earning male population was almost entirely wiped out in a single day. Only after decades of struggle would their children rebuild the community. It is no wonder that Chase and his pupils found willing paid models among the residents of the reservation, which today is more insular.

Sources: John Strong, "Sharecropping the Sea: Shinnecock Whalers in the Seventeenth Century," in Gaynell Stone, ed., *The Shinnecock Indians: A Culture History* (Stony Brook, New York: Suffolk County Archaeological Association, 1983), pp. 231–249. Carolyn Erland Brower, "The *Circassian* Story: 'We'll Float Tonight or We'll Go to Hell!'" with illustrations by David Bunn Siklos (Martine), ibid., pp. 367–399.

STAFF

Trudy C. Kramer
Director

Anke Jackson
Deputy Director

Alicia Grant Longwell
Curator of Art

Sally Briggs
Director of Development

Susan Jordan
Educator for Public Programs

Cara Conklin-Wingfield
Educator for School Programs

Erin Ferguson
Director of Public Relations

Nina Madison
Director of Special Events

Kenneth Johansson
Controller

Carol McCaffrey
Capital Campaign Director

Nanao Aqui
Museum Store Manager

Melinda Harrison
Director of Membership

Walter Gallagher
Building Manager

Christine McNamara
Registrar

Mary Slattery
Assistant Director of Special Events

Jennifer Kent
Assistant Educator

Kathleen Wik
Special Events Associate

Susan Swiatocha
Assistant for Finance

Becky Zaloga
Executive Assistant

Erik Davidowicz
Coordinator of Computer Systems

Novella Laspia
Curatorial Assistant

Kendra Owings
Special Events Assistant

Jennifer Rockford
Development Assistant

Winonah Warren
Public Relations Assistant

Will Davis
Assistant Building Manager

Ellen Kirwin
Clerical Assistant

Anne de Brigard
Receptionist

Laura Graham
Receptionist

Esther Siegel
Volunteer Coordinator

Adele Ray
Volunteer Coordinator

Designed by Bethany Johns
Printed in Germany by Cantz

Library of Congress Control Number:
2001089162

ISBN 0-943526-48-5

Cover:
William Merritt Chase, *The Bayberry Bush*, c. 1895.
Oil on canvas, 25 x 33 1/8 inches. The Parrish Art Museum, Littlejohn Collection.

PHOTOGRAPHY CREDITS

Cover and gatefold: Tim Lee. Page 7: Courtesy Cindy Sherman and Metro Pictures, New York. Pages 9, 29, 36–41, 59, 91, 93–95, 98, 101, 109, 111, 112: Noel Rowe. Pages 27, 65, 89, 103, 108: Gary Mamay. Page 43: Richard P. Meyer. Page 45: Mrs. Hudson's Fine Books and Päper, Chelsea, New York. Pages 49 (left), 58: Cathy Carver. Page 49 (right): Dorothy Zeidman. Page 56 (left): Elio Montanari. Page 56 (right): Taishi Hirokwa. Page 60: Courtesy Lehmann Maupin Gallery, New York. Page 62: Courtesy Gavin Brown's enterprise, New York. Page 66: Courtesy Cohan Leslie and Browne, New York. Page 68: Courtesy Klemens Gasser & Tanja Grunert, Inc., New York. Page 72 (left): Courtesy Pat Hearn Gallery, New York. Page 72 (right): Gabor Szitanyi. Page 74: Courtesy Lombard-Freid Fine Arts, New York. Pages 83, 84: Courtesy David Zwirner Gallery, New York. Page 90: Jonathan Wallen, from Samuel G. White, *The Houses of McKim, Mead & White* (New York: Rizzoli, with the Museums at Stony Brook, 1998).